Bill D. Schul

How to be an effective
GROUP LEADER

Nelson-Hall, Chicago

Library of Congress Cataloging in Publication Data

Schul, Bill D
  How to be an effective group leader.

  Bibliography: p.
  Includes index.
  1. Leadership. I. Title.
HM141.S38   301.15''53   74-31420
ISBN 0-911012-61-3

Manufactured in the United States of America

Contents

Introduction

Groups of people meeting to discuss their common problems, needs, fears, hopes, and aspirations have probably existed since the beginning of man's ability to communicate with verbal symbols. In recent years, the meeting of groups for the democratic interchange of ideas as a conscious process has become more prevalent. This is witnessed by the increased membership in churches, discussion groups, forums, service-giving agencies, service and civic clubs, professional fraternities and sororities, encounter and sensitivity groups, community centers, and a variety of youth organizations.

The organizations and groups to which a person belongs usually play an important role in his life, contributing to his education, his leisure, and providing a medium through which he can express his ideas and opinions to other people and learn from them. His need for these associations more than likely has increased due to the complexity of modern society. Smaller family units and compartmentalization of human responsibilities have increased the feelings of alienation in our technological society.

Furthermore, the growing complexities of society have become the responsibility of government, social agencies, institutions, and organizations, ranging from the neighborhood up to national and international levels. The demands in areas of problem-solving, education, and gaining public support foster a mushrooming number of committees, commissions, study groups, and workshops which call upon adults and youths from all walks of life to share in a large or small way the responsibility for making it a better world in which to live.

The success of any group, whether it be a Boy Scout troop, the public relations committee of the local PTA, or a commission named by the president to study a national problem, depends to a large extent on its leadership. Without strong and competent leadership, the most well-meaning group will be reduced to impotency or chaos.

Most of these groups are made up of volunteers, and their leaders, chosen from their ranks to serve as president, chairman, or whatever, are not professionally trained for their roles. It is to these persons—the youth who finds himself head of a school organization, the woman elected president of her professional sorority, and the man who, with little previous experience, is named chairman of a state commission—that this book is dedicated.

It is essentially a how-to-do-it text, covering the whys and wherefores, the dos and don'ts of leadership, the magic of leading groups.

For a number of years, I have been engaged in the training of both adults and youths to be group leaders. In my work with all types of groups, I have become increasingly aware of the need for a particular kind of book, one in which group leadership methods and techniques are explained in nontechnical terms, a book which takes the novice step-by-step toward competent leadership and which will, at the same time, provide the more experienced with a guide and a reminder. Long in search of such a text, I decided to write it myself.

In endeavoring to meet this need, I have tried to keep the focus on the countless untrained leaders who have assumed, or will assume, the responsibility for the leadership of a group of people—children, adolescents, adults or elderly people. I have attempted to present leadership training in clear, nonprofessional terminology. I have written about those items which are discussed with leaders when they ask, "What procedures must I know to lead a group? How do I go about it? Are there any guidelines I can follow?"

I have used considerable illustrative material which has evolved from my experience as a leader and my efforts to train others. I believe the cases used from my files and memory will be of use to readers.

1 / On being chosen leader

You have been elected to serve as a leader. You may be pleased about this and looking forward to the role. On the other hand, you may feel honored by being so named but anxious about the assignment and fearful that you will be unable to handle the job successfully. Bear in mind that any person selected to lead a group, club, committee, organization, lodge, or whatever, would likely feel much the same way. There is some comfort in the knowledge.

Some one or group selected you for leadership responsibility because they had confidence in your personal qualifications for leadership. You should not consider this confidence of others as a burden, for they do not expect perfection of you. Examine the qualities that others might have seen in you as a potential leader. How can these qualities be used to guide the group you will lead?

Accept the fact from the beginning that everything will not run smoothly. Don't fantasize problems but simply acknowledge to yourself that conflicts will occur, as they always do when persons of different opinions work together for common goals. Actually, we would not want matters any other way. If all members of the group

1

held a single opinion or belief, there wouldn't be any need for group action. As Walter Lippman once stated, "Where everyone thinks alike, no one thinks very much."

During some sessions, you will leave with a glow of satisfaction, while others will fill you with great discouragement. Accept these ups and downs as part of the game. You *will* make mistakes. Rest assured that even after many years of leading groups you will still make mistakes. The day you start expecting perfection will be the beginning of endless frustration and disappointment. You will move closer to effective leadership as long as you are able to learn from your mistakes.

You will find that what works successfully in one meeting, or with one group, may precipitate a crisis at another. Unfortunately, there are no blueprints showing what a leader might do from moment to moment. There are basic guidelines, however, that you can use to direct your course. And while there is no tidy formula, the purpose of this book is to provide a kind of basic guidance which will help you find your own solutions to leading your group.

What is leadership?

By way of defining leadership, we could say that it refers to that process whereby an individual guides, directs, or influences the thoughts, feelings, or behavior of other human beings. Better still, we might add that good leadership helps others to arrive at a better understanding of themselves, of others, of the issues at hand, and to use this greater understanding to accomplish whatever common goals brought the members of the group together.

Whether leadership is planned or unplanned, it always has a purpose and a goal. It is a process of human interaction. There can be no leadership without followers, but the relationship is only successful as long as the followers wish to follow the leader. The distinction is an important one. A leaderless society doesn't exist, for whenever two or more persons come together there is no such thing as uncontrolled, unrestricted, or uninfluenced behavior. The existence of any group is evidence of the willingness of the members to work together rather than alone toward a goal. Working together is a give and take business and the leader is the catalyst of the process. He is successful when the members find the group accomplishments greater than those which could have been achieved by individuals.

There are reasons to believe that some persons have greater natural tendencies for leadership than others, but there is sufficient experimental evidence to prove that leadership can also be created, trained, and developed in persons of normal intellectual ability and emotional stability and who are willing to make the effort to learn.

The leader is a person who, on the whole, best lives up to the standards or values of the group. If the leader fails to embody or depreciates these values, the group is likely to be confused and disorganized. In the matter of bestowing favors, the leader is careful not to be under obligation to any one member, and he generally gives out more favors than he receives. He takes his pay in accepted leadership. Understanding the relationship of the individual to the group, the leader is attuned to the will of the majority. The group seeks greater wisdom and vision in its leader than in other members, but the leader must also bear in mind that this wisdom must be distilled from the best efforts and ideas of individuals and the group as a whole. The task of the leader is to help each member of the group to give and receive from the group.

Examining your role

You may have played the role of leader in one group or another, but have now reached that point where you are no longer sure what, if anything, is being accomplished, or why members are reacting in certain ways. Perhaps you are asking yourself, "What is it that they want? What are we trying to do? Is it worthwhile? Do I really know what I am doing?"

Or, this may be your first experience as a leader and you have been asked to serve as committee chairman of a Boy Scout troop, or perhaps you have been elected president of your Rotary Club. For a number of years, you have been an active member of the organization and you feel proud to serve as this year's president. But as that day approaches, you begin to have feelings of doubt. "Should I make some introductory remarks? Will I handle the proceedings correctly? Will my nervousness be obvious?"

These feelings and the questions you ask of yourself are normal ones for any conscientious leader. As a matter of fact, it would be advisable to continue to examine your relationship to the group every so often, regardless of how long you remain in office and after handling of the meetings has become routine. A good leader takes inventory often.

Your anxieties are a natural reaction and come with the excitement of entering into a new adventure. When the day arrives when you can conduct a meeting or give a speech without at least a few butterflies in the stomach, that will be the day when you are completely indifferent to the task at hand. Many years ago when conducting my first statewide youth conference, I asked our keynote speaker, U. S. Senator Frank Carlson of Kansas, if he still felt his heart pound a little faster when it was his turn to speak. "Yes, thank God, I do," he said. "When I don't, I will know it is time for me to turn the podium over to someone else."

The group experience

It is generally accepted that what we are and what we will become depends largely on those with whom we associate. Throughout our lives we are participants of group activity whether at home, in school, church, work, or social and recreational activities. It is surprising how few of our activities are done alone.

As often stated, man is a social creature and he enjoys being with those persons who share his interests, likes, values, and goals. Sharing these with others makes life worthwhile. Your first group experience outside of the home was with the other children in your neighborhood. As you grew older, your contacts were broadened through the school and perhaps the church and your choice of companions increased. You became a member of some groups involuntarily because of your age and where you lived. You were drawn to other groups because of your interest in sports, music, drama, and so on. Most people today belong to several groups. They will have their particular friends but they will meet also with many other people because of specific interests and pursuits.

While our lives are spent with other people in groups of all sizes for a variety of purposes and reasons, formal and informal, these arrangements do not necessarily insure individual fulfillment and contentment. Successful relationships with others seldom occur without work, dedication, and sensitivity to their thoughts and feelings. This would seem to hold true whether the group is a family, a baseball team, a large corporation, or a nation. People who live in a democracy can best learn the democratic process by practicing it. Being able to function democratically with other people cannot be learned from books; it has to be experienced. In our groups, clubs, sororities, fraternities, lodges, churches, agencies, and organizations, we can learn how to share in the decision-making process, and how to take and delegate responsibility and fulfill goals. These shared experiences, the give and take, the failures and successes, conflicts and harmony, provide us with our concepts of democracy. Through our experiences with groups—from the gang of kids on the street to perhaps membership on the board of a giant corporation—we learn to live and work with others and make a contribution to our neighborhood and our community.

Serving as chairman of a committee or serving as the leader of some type of small group can help to initiate effective community leadership. Within such experiences the individual can take the first steps in learning the responsibilities of leadership. This does not mean that you should rush out immediately in search of a leadership role. It seldom works that way. But, if you are an active member of an organization, and are an enthusiastic worker, your chances of being cast in some kind of leadership role are imminent and if you accept, what you will learn will amply pay you for the energy you expend.

Attributes of a leader

What attributes do members seek in a leader? The specific responsibility of the leader, of course, depends to some extent on the type of organization. An informal discussion group will more than likely want the leader to serve more as a moderator than as a decision-maker. On the other hand, the Boy Scout committee will want the troop leader to establish and maintain certain rules and codes of behavior. In other cases, for example, the presidency of a local chapter of the Mental Health Association, the tasks of the leader are clearly set forth and the person filling this position knows that he must function within a certain structure. While these assignments and procedural tasks will be described in some detail later, there are some general characteristics of sound leadership which we can consider here.

In order to answer the question of what members want from you as their leader, ask yourself what you have sought from leaders. These characteristics might include the following:

1. A solid knowledge of and dedication to the history, goals, values, achievements, and current directions of the organization.

2. An ability to keep issues in focus and matters in perspective; to demonstrate emotional stability in time of stress and conflict.

3. To value the opinions of each member, to judge each on its merits alone and not be persuaded or intimidated by displays of emotion or aggressiveness.

4. A willingness to give credit to others and to accept the blame for failures without being overly dramatic or obvious.

5. A good sense of humor, the ability to keep meetings lively and interesting will contribute as much as anything to good attendance, morale, and overall achievement.

6. To find enjoyment in the meeting and be able to infect others with enthusiasm.

7. To be responsive to the individual members but to be firm when necessary in order that the members know where they stand.

Effective leadership does not automatically happen. It requires thought, study, and practice. While it may be true that some persons have a certain knack for leading others, chances are that their experiences have prepared them for leadership.

We sometimes hear people say, "She's a born musician," or "He's a born athlete." These people apparently have certain natural abilities that allow them to perform effectively and with apparent ease. But what is so often overlooked are the long, hard hours of practice, the mental and physical discipline that brought these people to the level of superior performance.

I attended high school and later college with a person who was branded a "natural quarterback" while still quite young and his performances eventually won him the rank of All-American. Yet, in some ways, he resented being tagged as a natural, because he earned every minute of his glory. While his less gifted teammates put in their scheduled time on the practice field, my friend worked out every moment he could spare. He kept himself in top physical condition all year long. He practiced passes with anyone who could catch them, studied the various plays and formations and their potential effectiveness. He studied other quarterbacks in action at every opportunity.

In the same sense, a natural leader can learn from practice, experimentation, and by using whatever resources are available to him. He should continue to ask himself why certain things that he did or said were either successful or not. One shouldn't hesitate to seek assistance from persons who can offer constructive criticism or suggest ways of handling certain kinds of problems.

Sources of help may include the program director of a local agency involved in group work, the field executive in the national organization, the district governor of the service club, the field representative of a university extension service, a scout executive, the director of religious education in the church, and so forth.

If such a person is not available through your own organization, you may be able to locate an experienced individual in some other organization.

There may be training courses within your agency or organization, or within the community. You may want to check with the local chamber of commerce, the college or university closest to you, adult training courses offered by public schools, the local Council of Social Agencies, the local unit of the National Jewish Welfare Board, Catholic Charities, the Council of Churches, the Y.M.C.A., and Y.W.C.A. and others. Some cities have now established central volunteer bureaus and these agencies sometimes conduct youth and adult leadership training courses.

Some of the larger churches conduct annual in-service training courses and periodic leaders' meetings for the exchange of ideas and experiences. Such meetings can be quite useful. If your church is not one that conducts such meetings, perhaps one of the churches that does can be persuaded to allow you at least to sit in.

If you can find the time, it might be advisable to attend meetings of other organizations for the purpose of observing their leaders in action. While doing this, keep in mind your own strengths and weaknesses so that you will not endeavor to mimic but rather develop your own style.

There are books and pamphlets which can be of help and articles examining theories and practice of leadership. Some of these sources explore the problems faced by leaders in working with various groups. A selected bibliography is included in this book.

Qualities of leadership

Before moving on to the specific tasks and problems of leadership, let's review some of the qualities of leadership generally accepted as essential.

Leadership has been defined as the capacity and will to rally men and women to a common purpose. In order to be able to do this, self-confidence is necessary. People find it difficult to follow a leader who does not believe in himself. A leader must have sufficient energy to do anything he or she asks of members, and probably more. A real leader must be able to work harder, carry the greater responsibility, and go the extra mile.

There is also the important matter of timing, which is a combination of foresight, alertness, and imagination. "No man thinking thoughts born out of time," wrote Woodrow Wilson, "can succeed in leading his generation." General Mark W. Clark noted in a Reader's Digest article several years ago that Wilson's own career was a dramatic proof of the virtue of correct timing. "He led the United States into World War I when the country was ready for it, not before. But later, when Wilson pressed for U.S. participation in the

League of Nations, the country was not ready, and his effort ended in crashing failure. Same leader, same country—but wrong timing."

A leader must demonstrate clear-headed thinking. He must be able to reason logically, weigh alternatives, and make decisions. Above all, he must be able to convey his thoughts clearly.

Courage is always essential. It has been defined as the capacity to hang on five minutes longer than anyone else. Not only does the leader need to possess this ability himself, he must also inspire it in others. While we oftentimes identify courage as the capacity to face danger, closer examination reveals that it is tenacity, put to the test every time we face a difficult problem and are willing to see it through. When we stick by our beliefs regardless of how awkward and stressful this may be; when we can face up to mistakes without excusing ourselves or endeavoring to disguise them; when we can go on regardless of how tired we may be, and do so without complaint or boasting; when we tackle today's jobs today instead of putting them off until tomorrow, we *are* courageous.

There are times when a leader should be bold and assertive. Akin to courage, but more dynamic, boldness reveals itself in one's willingness to take chances and to reject the thought of failure. For example, a number of years ago I was elected president of our Lions Club. At the time, the membership was suffering, attendance was poor, and there was little enthusiasm for the club's activities. Something was needed, some project that would appear overwhelming, but which would provide the members with a genuine challenge, demanding the best in all. "Let's make it or break it," I thought. If the members could become excited and rally to a cause, then we would be a club again, have pride, the respect of the community, but more important, a renewed belief in ourselves.

It was well-known in the community that the high school had long wanted an electric scoreboard for the football stadium. The school board didn't feel it could spend the money, but people went on saying how much a scoreboard was needed. First, a women's club and then one of the service clubs tried to raise the money but their efforts had been to no avail. It was this project that I presented to the membership. There were gasps, references to the failures by other organizations, and suggestions for smaller projects. But the members knew, as well as I did, that a small project wouldn't accomplish our goals. In the end, they rallied to the cause, and how they rallied! Pancake fries, auctions, amateur vaudeville shows, and a huge thermometer on Main Street let everyone know how we were faring. There was no turning back then.

It took us four months but we made it. In its wake there was pride, self-assurance, tremendous enthusiasm for the club, and an increase in membership. Looking back, I am sure that this experience did as much for us as individuals as it did for the club.

A leader needs to be concerned. My experience has been that people will not follow a leader for very long unless they feel that the leader truly cares about them and is sympathetic to their problems and needs.

A leader also needs to display a strong sense of personal morality. Unless a leader knows where he stands, what to him is right and wrong, and is able to live up to his ideals, he will not long be a leader. A person who knows who he is and where he is going, and yet does not force his values on others, has the kind of inner poise that naturally draws others to him.

Perhaps above all else, a leader must have faith, a belief in himself and his people as well as the goal toward which he is leading them.

2 / Preparing for leadership

Developing magnetism

A group of highly skilled behaviorial scientists attended a seven-state meeting in Omaha, Nebraska during the Spring of 1971 to develop techniques for implementing the recommendations of the 1970 White House Conference on Children and Youth. They were professional men and women—psychiatrists, psychologists, sociologists, attorneys, judges, social workers—all well-educated and experienced. Each of the participants stated his or her views fluently. The meeting was inundated with intellectualism. But it was getting nowhere. Some ingredient, a magnetism of some sort, was needed to pull this group together and give it new life.

It appeared for a time that the conference might come to a close with little accomplished. The representatives of the federal government were showing signs of distress; they might have to return to Washington with an empty bag despite their elaborate planning. Suddenly a short, nondescript-looking man jumped to his feet. His clothes didn't fit him especially well and were by no means in the latest style. The participants seemed mildly curious about his appearance and behavior—at first. But, as he spoke, rapidly and forcefully, his speech colored by rural colloquialisms, the dignified participants listened attentively. Within two minutes, this small man had the group in the palm of his hand.

Why? He was the first one to radiate enthusiasm! The intellectuals had radiated dignity and bearing but no sparks.

This country bumpkin, with his drawl and slang, sparkled with fire and interest and concern. He lacked bearing, looks, and eloquent speech, but he had an abundance of what the others lacked—magnetism. A farmer and rancher, he had become interested in state and national planning for children and youth because he believed that lay citizens should have a voice in planning efforts and proposed legislation. He was there not because his job required it but because of genuine interest, and he was not about to let the meetings close without some positive action. He electrified the group with his personal magnetism. His appeals and suggestions became the turning point in the meetings. Concrete steps were taken for implementation of the recommendations and national chairman Stephen Hess later told me that this had been the best of the area meetings.

After attending this meeting, I found myself thinking about the little farmer and it occurred to me that personal magnetism is the most important quality that a leader of any group, young or old, can possess. Thinking of my own experiences with groups and talking with all kinds of leaders, I concluded that there are certain qualities that electrify others and, secondly, that they can be learned and practised.

The first characteristic of magnetism is one of activity. All magnetic people are active. They wear out their shoes, not their trousers. They stand up when they could sit down; they move when they might stand still. You do not need to be born with this love of activity but you can practise being more active.

Dwight Eisenhower is a case in point. He made himself active and when alone would be relaxed and retiring. When with people, however, he took on an active manner, moved with intensity and spoke with vigor.

A trained actress cultivates this characteristic and can steal scenes from beautiful women who lack vigor and involvement. The story is told of Charlotte Cushman who started singing in opera. Then something happened to her voice and she had to give up singing. Undaunted, she worked at developing another talent and became an outstanding dramatic actress. She was not beautiful, no longer had an operatic voice, but she knew how to involve an audience.

Magnetic people are enthusiastic when they speak. They often speak rapidly. Listen to radio and television news commentators and repeat the words after them. You will notice that their voices go up slightly at the end of sentences, which helps to keep listeners expectant. When your voice trails off, you lose listeners. Keep your voice exciting, end a thought with a certain emphasis, and you will keep their attention.

Special emphasis is given certain words by magnetic speakers. They are conscious of timing, pausing for a split second, and drawing attention to that pause, and following with a careful attention drawn to each word. If you were fortunate enough to have heard Winston Churchill speak, you may have recognized that one of the secrets of his powerful magnetism was a lack of a monotone in his speech pattern. When he spoke, one could almost imagine a band playing in the background.

You do not need to have a musical voice to develop a quality of magnetic speech. To a large extent, you were born with your voice, but this is not what determines the magnetism; it is the ways in which you use your voice. Make it an active and concerned voice. Involve your audience with your own concern and enthusiasm.

A second quality you may wish to cultivate is that of briskness. The world-famous psychiatrist Karl Menninger is deliberately brisk without appearing brusque. He has a very active handshake but a brief one. He stops while the other person still expects one more vigorous pump of the hand. Dr. Menninger's speech is brisk and businesslike. He will talk actively for a short time and then stop, allowing others to continue the conversation. His glance is brisk and appraising. For a few seconds, he gazes intensely into another person's eyes and then his glance may drop to their hands.

Dr. Menninger displays this quality at meetings and social gatherings. He is usually one of the first to leave. While he is there, one cannot help but be conscious of his presence. He is friendly, warm, and he moves actively about the room. Then suddenly, without lingering, he leaves, while the others are still expectant.

Interviews, whether you are interviewing someone or they you, should be brief, and this can be accomplished without offending people. When someone is in your office, you may wish to glance at your watch and stand up to indicate that it is stopping time. A friend of mine lays down his pipe when someone enters his office, and when he decides that the discussion has reached its conclusion, he picks up his pipe again.

I keep a sign in my office, "Time is precious. Don't waste it." I believe this helps. It is posted where visitors cannot possibly overlook it.

Most interviews should be brief. Lengthy interviews go in circles, anyway. To break away from an interview does not need to be an awkward gesture and no excuses are needed. When you know that it's time for you to leave, stand up and say, "I have to go now," and then go. Don't linger, talking all the way to the door. Pay your respects and keep on moving. When you fail to be brief, you soon become a bore, a quality a leader can ill afford.

One of the most important habits to cultivate is cheerfulness. Will Rogers was loved by an entire world because of his cheerfulness and an ability to find humor in things that other people worried about.

You cannot have personal magnetism without being cheerful. This requires you to be optimistic and to encourage others and to minimize pessimism in yourself and others. Despite the problems, you should talk success and not failure. To be magnetic, you may at times have to practice cheerfulness when you don't feel it. The amazing thing is, however, that pretending cheerfulness often works and infects others.

A business friend of mine has had sufficient illness and financial setbacks to sink most people. Yet he is one of the most cheerful people I know. "What good would it do to linger over my losses?" he asked. "It certainly wouldn't contribute to solutions."

Another necessary quality of the leader is directness. When you speak, speak directly to people and not to the ceiling or the floor or the back of the room. A few years ago I worked with a young man in the planning of several statewide youth conferences. He was extremely sharp, tall, and good-looking. He expressed himself well, but he had developed the habit of speaking in a low monotone, allowing his voice to drift away from his audience. He also had the bad habit of never looking directly at people as he spoke to them. After I had become well-acquainted with him, I called these things to his attention and offered to help him overcome these unattractive habits. I was pleased when he accepted my offer and in a very short time, he no longer needed coaching. Not long ago I received a letter from him while attending the University of Wyoming. He had been elected president of his class.

When you look out of the window as you speak, you are not being direct. But notice that when others look at you directly (which has escaped you if you have been looking at the floor), there is a certain spark that comes along with the words. You should be direct whether you are speaking or listening.

A friend of mine, who had spent forty years training salespeople, told me that one of the most common faults of beginning salesmen is looking at the goods they are displaying rather than looking at the customers. You've heard people say that so and so has magnetic eyes. Chances are, however, that his or her eyes are about the same as other people's, a little smaller than some and a little larger than others. All eyes become magnetic when they are focused directly on one. The look in the eye of the true leader, the one who has power over people, is one of honesty and directness.

While some people may be brilliant and accomplished, they cannot exercise effective leadership because they lack magnetism. They simply are not very exciting.

Fearlessness

There is still another leadership quality which, surprisingly enough, can also be practised and learned, and that is courage or fearlessness. Truly, heroes are made, not born. The person who makes a practice of straddling the fence because he is fearful of crossing will find few followers in any camp.

Playing it safe, going with the majority, usually wins nothing but contempt. One cannot behave like a rubber stamp, displaying a lack of character and individuality, and also be a leader. To radiate magnetism, one also has to express opinions and have a mind of one's own. To lead, one has to stand by his convictions, to be willing to fight for what he or she thinks is right.

The leader needs to be fearless in thought, words, and action. People respect and respond to fearlessness. Ever notice how animals react to fear? Mount a horse with a feeling of fear and you discover an unruly horse. Run from a barking dog and he will chase you, but walk up to him and he will either wag his tail or he will run. Such approaches will work as well with people. Even when we don't feel very brave, it pays to display courage anyway.

Stories have been told of Teddy Roosevelt's prowess with his fists, of decking more than one challenger. On one such occasion some of his political rivals hired an underworld muscleman known as Stubby Collins to beat up Roosevelt in the Delavan House in Albany. Collins tried to earn his pay but a few moments after attacking Roosevelt he was stretched out cold.

Physical courage is a virtue, but of even greater importance is moral courage. To be a leader, one must be willing to fight for one's ideals with as much energy as one would fight for his life. Politicians have won office by satisfying various factions, but few have won high offices and retained them without defense of their own principles.

Developing poise

A quality that is sometimes overlooked because in some ways it is a product of other qualities is poise. Poise is that quality that allows you to be criticized without getting mad, that lets you laugh at yourself, that helps to keep you calm in emergencies, that allows you to speak in public without an outward display of nervousness, that keeps you going when things are turning out badly.

Poise is no more a natural trait than bravery or honesty. Its existence, or lack of it, can become a habit. As with other personal characteristics, poise doesn't just happen. It requires effort. But if you are willing to take on the responsibility of an organization, group, company, or whatever, you are not one who avoids self-improvement.

While no one expects a college graduating class to demonstrate the kind of poise they may eventually display after being out in the world a few years, nevertheless, they are no longer adolescents and one expects some poise from them. But attending a college graduating ceremony recently, I was amazed at the display of nervous mannerisms of the graduates.

But then the faculty members were doing little better. One was a tie player. His tie looked fine but every so often he would adjust it. Another kept smoothing the back of his hair even though it was lying flat. One woman wiped her glasses at least four times. On stage, two members of the board of trustees couldn't seem to face the audience. They studied every inch of the ceiling. Throughout the room were nose-rubbers, ear-pullers, finger-twisters, scratchers, and foot-tappers.

All of the above things are a matter of habit and good habits can replace bad ones if one works at it. An absence of poise is evidence of negligence. There are exercises one can practice to gain greater poise.

Forget yourself

We spend too much time thinking about ourselves. Young people are sometimes misled into believing that they can make the opposite sex immediately fall for them by concentrating on being physically attractive. It just doesn't work out that way. People fall in love because they have a real need and genuine respect and love for another person, because that other person provides a sense of well-being. If you want someone to be interested in you, be genuinely interested in him or her. When you become important to him or her, he or she will be more interested in you. This approach applies to all relationships with others, whether we wish them to like us, hire us, promote us, or elect us president. It requires forgetting yourself and being genuinely interested in others.

A friend of mine once did a study to ascertain why some college girls were more popular than others. He discovered that the popular girls were those who were poised and self-confident. For example, when a confident girl was introduced to a boy, she did not need to keep asking herself, "Do I look all right? Will I say the right things?" Rather, she would concentrate on how he was feeling and how she could make him more comfortable. Of course he liked that and, because he did, he liked her; being liked, she felt more confident than ever and was even better meeting people the next time. Her popularity grew and grew.

I once knew a young man named Paul who had a date with Joan for the Junior Prom. He was looking forward to the event and was very excited about it. But on the morning of the dance, Joan's mother telephoned that Joan was sick with the flu. Paul was heartbroken.

Living in the same apartment house as Paul was Kathleen, a smart, attractive career woman of about twenty-two. Kathleen had many dates, but usually when a man brought her home, he would say good night and that would be the last time she would see him. Kathleen, not having a date for that particular evening, offered to go to the dance with Paul. When they returned home after the dance, Paul was completely head-over-heels in love with Kathleen. And, yet, the following evening when Kathleen dated a man closer to her own age, he told her good night and she never heard from him again.

What happened? Why was Kathleen so influential with Paul and not with the older man? Well, when Kathleen went to the prom with Paul, she did everything within her power to see that he had a good time. She listened to every word he told her and told him what a great athlete he was, and when he paid her a compliment, she thanked him and returned the conversation to him. She gave him recognition and the kind of social security Joan probably would have been unable to do.

But when Kathleen dated older men, she expected them to meet *her* needs. And she told herself that what they probably wanted was a cool, impressive, glamour girl. She was wrong, for most men need someone to meet their needs, to provide security, and to discover that what they say is important. All of the beautiful clothes, make-up, and hair-styles are of little use unless a person displays an interest in others.

A young attorney faced the prospects of giving up trial work although he wanted very much to be a trial lawyer. He was brilliant and had infinite patience for detailed research, but he would lose all of his poise in the courtroom. Easily upset, he was so self-conscious that he constantly toyed with his clothes, pushed at his hair and looked past the judge and the jury. His opponents soon learned to take advantage of his weaknesses.

Reminders

I know a legislator who uses a talisman to remind him to maintain his poise. His talisman is an Irish good-luck coin which he carries in his pocket or holds in his hand when he is speaking. He has instructed himself in the use of the coin. He has told himself that the coin will always remind him to remain poised, regardless of the challenge or irritations, especially that he must never be pushed into saying something he would not wish to say.

Although he is not superstitious, he makes the coin do its bit of magic. Given to him years ago by a friend, the coin lay in a dresser drawer until one day while dressing for a particularly pressing day before the legislature, when it would be necessary for him to stage a fight for an important bill, he rediscovered the coin. He picked it up, saying, "If I ever needed you, it's today." He thought about what he would need to do that day to win passage of his bill. He told himself that the coin would remind him to keep his poise. He performed magnificently that day, his resolution was passed, and the coin has remained close to him ever since.

A private prop can sometimes work miracles; it can help center us upon a necessary focal point. The young attorney's talisman was a business card on the back of which he had written, "Study Others." It reminded him to forget himself by focusing his attention on others. He didn't have to take the card out and read it. He knew what it said but feeling it in his pocket reminded him of its message.

There are all kinds of talismans. School diplomas and awards, certificates of membership in professional groups, union cards can all serve as good-luck pieces because they give us confidence in and remind us of our achievements. The presence of certain books in an office or study, or the copy of a poem or saying posted in plain sight can also serve as a talisman.

There is an old saying about putting your brain in gear before your tongue. If followed, it would go a long way toward helping you to maintain your poise. In psychology, it is called "the delayed response." When upset, we are cautioned to count to ten before speaking.

While smoking a pipe may contribute little to my physical health, I believe fiddling with a pipe has helped me to maintain my equilibrium. When I have been asked a question and I need to gain some time before I answer, my pipe buys me that time. I strike a match and slowly take a few drags while I collect my thoughts. Apparently others do not question this—it seems like a normal thing to do. I am not suggesting that anyone take up pipe-smoking. This is "my thing" and I am sure you can develop some calculated delays of your own and perhaps much more healthful ones.

What I am suggesting is that you let no one or situation force you to rush into impulsive and imprudent answers. Anything worth saying is worth thoughtful consideration. And I think it is safe to say that most of the world's great leaders do their thinking before they speak. To be poised, you must learn to do much of your thinking in advance. Envision yourself in conversation or speaking before a group and see if you can imagine all kinds of problems occurring and envision yourself handling those problems—with poise and presence.

When you learn to do your thinking in advance and can plan for emergencies *before* they happen, you will gain considerable poise. You lose your poise when you are not prepared for the unexpected. Always take time to collect your thoughts. Even if you are in the middle of a speech and you need a moment to think, take it. Pause silently but by all means don't stall around with any "well-uhs."

Breathe slowly

The Indian practice of yoga has grown popular in this country recently. Its practitioners seek control over the body mechanisms and brain, and early in their exercises they are taught to control their breathing. According to the yoga system, control of the body and mind depends upon control of breathing, and it is said that in order to gain inner poise and tranquillity, one must learn to slow down respiration. Breathing exercises are also in widespread use now in psychotherapy. It has been discovered that an emotionally upset person can gain relief by learning to slow down the respiratory process.

When people are excited, under stress, and have lost their poise, they breathe rapidly and take in little oxygen. Notice the next time that you feel nervous or anxious how fast you are breathing. Slow down your breathing by taking deliberate and deep inhalations and exhalations. I think you will be amazed how quickly you will feel better and more at ease. This is of particular help when you are nervous before a meeting over which you must preside or before you give a talk. You can practice deep breathing even if you are on stage. Simply become conscious of your breathing and deliberately slow it down.

Have you ever noticed that when people get excited their voices start to rise? This always happens when the breathing rate increases. So you may wish to tune in on your own voice from time to time. When it is higher than usual, pitch it lower while you also breathe more slowly. When at all possible, find a quiet room in which to hold your meeting so that you will not have to raise your voice to make yourself heard. If a choice of a room or auditorium is not possible, move the group or audience as close to you as possible. Then you will be able to maintain your poise much more easily.

Need for conviction

True personal magnetism is never superficial. All the charm in the world in the end is empty unless it radiates a firm conviction of the individual leader, a conviction that also imbues followers with confidence. Each group must have faith in itself but it also needs support. A conference leader wants to make sure that out of group conference a harmonizing of human thoughts will evolve. A trade association executive wants assurance that there will be more cooperation within his industry and less need for competition. The PTA chairman must honestly believe that the schools will be enhanced by the greater involvement of parents. The labor union leader must have faith in the process of collective bargaining. The Boy Scout leader must believe that the activities of the organization foster healthy values in youth. A service club president must have faith in compassion and generosity to those less fortunate. Where strong faith in a particular effort is present and is imparted to others, it also generates mutual enthusiasm.

I feel certain that in order to be a strong leader, you need to believe there is inherent value in human life; that mankind struggles, not against, but essentially in harmony with the universe. The best leaders have faith that human nature has a great potentiality for growth. Only when leaders have such faith do they possess the power to inspire others.

As a leader you have to be willing to trust people and give them responsibility. You must act on the assumption that when people are committed, they will usually work hard. This is not to say that, as a leader, you will never need to renew members' enthusiasm and summon them to greater endeavor. The response from most people is unbelievably great if only the leader knows how to tap their resources.

People stand ready to be summoned but the cause must be clearly recognizable to them. It's important that they feel they are being called upon to realize new levels of achievement. My experience has led me to believe that people will respond to appeals for greater accomplishment if their leaders have faith in them. This is particularly true today when most people have to express themselves largely through various organized group activities.

In the final analysis, one of two philosophies of life can be held. Either life can be viewed as if it had meaning and therefore that human endeavor can make a contribution toward the realization of that meaning, or life can be interpreted as having no meaning, in which case all human effort is futile. I think you will find few people who consistently act as if life had no meaning. But there are plenty of people who think that they believe something like this. It's called existentialism. Such a philosophy, however unconscious, is certainly not one to be held by a leader. A leader is essentially a believer, an affirmer, a doer, and creator. He believes that goals can be realized and that human energy can be constructively directed, that events can be molded.

3 / Influencing others

The knowledge of the processes involved in influencing people has increased considerably in recent years. The leader's use of that knowledge is actually a matter of recognizing and applying these behaviors in daily life.

Some of the most important of these processes are: (1) imitation; (2) suggestion; (3) exhortation; (4) persuasion; (5) publicity; (6) reliance upon the logic of events; (7) the demonstration of devotion. It is difficult to generalize as to the particular times when you, as a leader, should use one or more of these methods. Usually several of these influences are in operation at the same time. However, an awareness of how each works can be helpful.

Imitation

Imitation is not an active process exercised on the group by the leader. As we have seen with youth gangs in our large cities, the members of the group will oftentimes imitate the leaders' phrases, mannerisms, clothing, and lifestyle. This also has occurred with members of fan clubs of movie idols and sports heroes. These become identifying factors within the group, providing a sense of unity and familiarity. While we cannot overlook the importance of these aids, particularly when working with youth, it is a shallow leader who places too strong a reliance upon the forces of imitation to assist him in achieving group unity.

Once an organization or a program within an organization has been soundly established and has a following, it becomes the thing to do to join the leader and his group and/or to imitate them. Nothing succeeds better than success, of course, because people will always copy or follow those with success and status.

Suggestion

There may be either a direct or indirect form of suggestion, very often a hint designed to enhance the leader's status in the eyes of the members. This occurs when the leader indicates that there are some wealthy, powerful or prominent supporters of the organization. An example might be a letter received from a senator or well-known athlete. Using "names" on the board of directors or a list of prominent citizens on an advisory council are typical maneuvers for reinforcing the importance of the leader or the organization.

In order to gain prestige, some leaders will resort to honorific titles, special uniforms or dress, impressive offices, being inaccessible, and dramatic public appearances. Occasionally the reverse will be used, with the leader going out of his way to impress people that he is just one of the boys. Such gestures as the mayor driving a truck during a city clean-up drive or a politician using terms or phraseology spoken by the group with which he is associating are examples at efforts to be seen as a regular guy.

Suggestion can be used effectively if you wish the members to take some action but you prefer that they do this on their own rather than at your direction. The power of suggestion will usually result in action if the leader is willing to allot sufficient time for it to develop. One of the gravest faults of leaders is to overuse their capacity for getting things done quickly. Think carefully about this, if you are contemplating some form of action. It may be preferable for the members to take the initiative. People are more supportive and protective of ideas which they conceive of as being their own. In order to get the ball rolling, you may at times wish to plant a seed and give others the chance to nurture it. I have seen many leaders lose the support of their followers by rushing ahead when greater wisdom would have told them to hand the ball to others.

The power of suggestion can be seen in the hints which people pass along to one another. A negative suggestion such as, "I understand that he drinks rather heavily," or "Well, if you ask me, I think his honesty is suspect," can really hurt a leader even when there is not a bit of truth in such statements. Positive ones, on the other hand—"If he belongs to the group, that's good enough for me," "He's got my vote"—can go a long way in converting others.

Constant suggestion has a profound effect on people's views. The use of a symbol, a slogan, a creed, song, are reminders and it is known that they can be powerful thought conditioners.

The advertising industry has long been aware that conditioning the subconscious mind and appealing to emotions is more important than what is acceptable to the rational or conscious mind. As a leader, however, you may wish to use constructively suggestions which appeal to various special-interest groups. A leader can use whatever symbols, slogans, or sayings are relevant to the organization. To appeal to the subconscious minds of the members, you may wish to repeat such phrases as "community service" or "be prepared" in your talks, on your stationery, and so forth. But in the long run, the best leadership is supported by feelings among the followers that the objectives being served are reasonable and rational.

Exhortation

Preaching, oratory, and lecturing are all forms of exhortation frequently used in religion, politics, and education. How valuable such public discourses are for influencing others it is difficult to measure. But the retention of this method throughout history would seem to indicate some value. Certainly speech in the hands of a gifted orator can impart excitement and bring others to a point of emotional fervor and enthusiasm. To what extent it imparts information of a more lasting nature as compared to the printed word is debatable, but most scholars contend that the printed word has a greater and more lasting influence as it can be referred to again and again.

When oratory is employed for its emotional impact rather than for intellectual appeal, it fails to sustain conviction and enthusiasm over long periods of time. Human emotions are incapable of prolonged expression without the repetition of the stimulus which arouses them.

A speech or an oration with an intellectual content will also be remembered if it relates to concerns close to the listeners' lives. A familiar phrase, the use of anecdotes to illustrate points, the graphic presentation of concrete ideas, usually offered at the beginning and the conclusion of a speech, will contribute to the success of the presentation. Thanks to today's mass communication, particularly television, people are much more sophisticated now than a generation or two ago and the proverbial expansive, but empty, clichés of political and religious oratory are of the past.

Persuasion

The most common and the most effective tool for the influencing of others is persuasion by argument. The ability to use sound arguments, to be able to explore all possible alternatives, to weigh the issues, and to be able to articulate your views at meetings of the membership, board meetings, and committee discussions will be a great asset to you as a leader. Perhaps you have had little practice in persuasive argument. This, then, is where some of the exercises we have mentioned—keeping your poise, deep breathing, directing your thoughts away from yourself, the use of a talisman, doing your thinking in advance, and so forth—will serve their turn. And by all means do your homework. You will be much better prepared for any arguments which may arise if you are soundly versed in the issues and have already thought of the pros and cons.

Publicity

The use of publicity to influence people serves little purpose in a small group where each member is acquainted with one another and with the activities of the organization. Publicity, however, can be extremely useful to build prestige, to educate, interpret facts, and report on activities to a large membership and to the public at large.

Many corporations, foundations, associations, institutions, and agencies publish magazines or newsletters to inform both their members and the interested public. If your group does not have a newsletter, you might wish to give this some thought.

If your group is a local chapter of a state or national organization, you will benefit from the publicity of the parent organization. For your group to be included in the state or national publication, it will be necessary for you to report on activities and projects. Usually the reports are handled by the local publicity chairman, or, if none exists, you may wish to appoint someone.

Do not imagine for a moment that publicity can be handled by just anyone in the group. Good publicity, or the lack of it, can be extremely important to a group, particularly one that depends upon public support. Pick for your publicity chairman a person who is enthusiastic, informed, and can exercise good judgment. It helps if the publicity chairman has had some experience and is acquainted with the news media.

Your choice of media and methods of publicity depend largely on the purposes of the group and the nature of your activities. A large, well-known organization may have access to abundant newspaper coverage, radio, and television time. But, regardless of the size of your group and its importance in the community, most radio stations will provide you with at least some public service time, and the newspapers will probably give you space even though it may be on the back page. Don't let this discourage you. Keep working at activities worthy of coverage and use your personal magnetism and matters are bound to improve.

Printed handbills announcing meetings can be used if they are posted in places where they will attract sufficient attention. Printing extra newsletters and sending them to a selected mailing list of non-members can also be effective. Another successful method of publicity is the personal letter. Nothing is more appealing, with the exception of a personal visit, than receiving a letter directed to you personally. The form letter can sometimes be used, but don't expect it to get the results of the personal letter.

The logical moment

There will be times, while serving as a leader, when you will feel you must wait for certain events to take place before members of your group can be made aware of a problem. More than likely, you will be more conscious of the problem or the issue than they and you may be able to look ahead and plan imaginatively certain steps. But remember that you may become discouraged when you discover that few of your followers can manifest that kind of vision. Most people worry about problems or take action when they can no longer be ignored. But when you see the handwriting on the wall, you must decide whether or not to force the attention of the members to these imminent issues or to await the unfolding of events to bring members' awareness of the problems.

Watchful waiting, of course, is part of the business of being a leader, and only experience itself can teach you when affirmative action is necessary. Speaking in a very general way, however, I would venture to say that the virtue lies in making every effort to inform your members as early as possible about issues, problems, troubles, or whatever, for that matter. There are always exceptions. One of these is when you are an adult serving as a leader or sponsor of a children's or youth organization. Obviously, there will be issues which they will be unable to understand. Let us say that you are sponsor of a church youth center and you have been told by the board of trustees that the center may have to be closed because of the lack of funds. You appeal to the board by saying that you would be willing to conduct a fund raising drive. The board replies, however, that its policy is to raise funds for all of the church's activities and not to conduct separate campaigns. You hope to change this policy, however, and decide not to mention the problem to the young people until the matter is at least resolved with the board of trustees.

Devotion

The leader's devotion to the members of the group is a positive and dynamic force and the group's response is generally one of devotion to the leader. No single factor exercises greater influence over people than one of genuine and meaningful devotion.

Vince Lombardi, the late legendary coach of the Green Bay Packers, was probably the hardest taskmaster ever to step on the gridiron. But his team won championships mostly because of his faith in and devotion to each of the players as individuals. In turn, the players would play their hearts out for him. As Jerry Kramer, former star of the Green Bay Packers, explained recently on one of the late talk shows, "It was more important to be seen as a good football player in Coach Lombardi's eyes than to win any other honors. We would win because we didn't want to let him down."

When teams win ball games, when workers go the extra mile without additional wages, when an orchestra plays better than usual, when students overachieve, and volunteers perform beyond the call of duty, the super effort can usually be attributed to a devotion to the leader. Of such a leader you will hear people say, "I would do anything for him or her."

Check the record of any great man who succeeded in a large way—Abraham Lincoln, Martin Luther King, George Washington, Alexander the Great, Gandhi—and you will discover that they had the ability to win the devotion of large numbers of people. How you can be the kind of leader who evokes a deep devotional response from others is a question that, as a student of leadership, you will wish to continually ask yourself. You will gain the devotion of others only if you first can demonstrate this kind of devotion. Secondly, you cannot break the faith or misplace the loyalty of your followers. They do not expect you to be perfect but they will expect you to place their welfare ahead of your own, at least within the scope and context of the organization.

The capacity for affection varies from person to person. Some are more warm and friendly, energetic and extroverted individuals than others. They are good mixers and seem to have a certain sweep and force to their personalities. These people are usually generous and sympathetic, display warmth and directness which quickly creates rapport with most people. They usually find little or no difficulty in expressing affection.

To what extent this outward display of personality can be cultivated, it is difficult to say. In any case, there are plenty of successful leaders who are not able to be openly demonstrative. Some people, including leaders, are just naturally shy and find it difficult to display much emotion, yet by their actions demonstrate how they feel.

I think it would be well to remember that the true source of power and influence comes from the heart. It is passion, passion for truth that marks the great philosopher; passion for justice which distinguishes the jurist; passion for beauty which unfolds in the finest artists. And always, a person will be judged by what he does rather than what he says.

As a leader, it is important that you clearly understand why affection is so potent a force. Affection, for our purposes, can be defined as an ability to identify with others, to feel genuine empathy, and consciously to work for the well-being and happiness of others.

Affection is essential for the leader as it predisposes more people to being influenced. People will do many things for those who care for them. They will endeavor to live up to their expectations. Fulfilling such expectations gives us a great deal of pleasure for we feel needed. Affection is a powerful motivating force.

More often than not, the leader should not expect affection. But if he or she is a devoted and successful leader, affection will be lavished upon him. So many human lives are emotionally impoverished and seldom moved by genuine feelings of affection. Many people, fearful of being rejected and hurt, build walls around themselves. They are hesitant of reaching out to others, to committing themselves to persons and causes. Some people distrust themselves and therefore distrust others. They guard against being stirred or emotionally caught up in relationships with other people and, yet, this is what they yearn for the most.

It is not so surprising, then, that people will lavish a considerable amount of affection on the leader who can show them the way toward a worthwhile goal and who cares for them as individuals.

Such devotion, of course, places a great deal of responsibility upon the leader. Unless intelligently used, affection can degenerate into mere sentimentality: personal attachment on the part of the leader and something close to uncritical idolatry on the part of the followers.

How can meaningful affection be developed for more effective leadership?

As a rule, affection is a very personal experience. Usually we feel affection for those we know and our closest friends are those with whom we share common interests and goals. Universal love of mankind is not easily attained. Even love of the community does not come automatically. The lover of a group of people, a state, a nation, of humanity, comes with maturity which many people never acquire. It grows from love of family, friends, a growing circle of neighbors; it has its roots in local interests. It widens as the individual's sensitivity, experience, knowledge, and understanding of others increase. Such affection takes imagination and effort.

It is not terribly difficult to convince parents of the need for a new school building. But it is somewhat harder to arouse people to do something for starving children in another country.

By way of working at developing more affection for others, you must make a deliberate effort to become interested in the members as individuals. You should learn their names, where they work or go to school, and what their interests are. If you are not outgoing by nature, you must practice the habit of responding to others. In order to cultivate this habit, it is necessary to practice it with everyone you contact—elevator operators, waitresses, cab drivers, secretaries, janitors, coworkers, whomever—with a friendly "Good morning," and so on. It is very important to people to be noticed and you will be amazed how differently they will respond to you when you recognize their existence as individuals.

To be aware of others takes effort but it pays big dividends. The fact that you are reading these words would indicate that you are now serving, or plan to serve, in some capacity as a leader. That being the case, people are now your business. You will receive from them pretty much what you give them.

One of the more common oversights for a person making initial efforts to expand his or her awareness is to regard only the members present and forget about those who aren't there. While action cannot be suspended until all members are present and accounted for, the leader should at least be conscious of the wishes and needs of those who are absent. A leader can sometimes lose the support of members by appointing to committees only those present, or planning some project affecting all members but which is designed by a small minority of the membership. If the project or program is of some importance, every effort should be made to insure their attendance or tap their opinions. Then, if they do not respond, they have no one to blame but themselves. A regard for those present to the neglect of those absent is more common than you might imagine.

Affection is developed and nurtured by a deliberate habit of expressing solicitude for others. Affection grows as personal contact continues and is reciprocated. It deepens as the leader expands his relationship to nonmembers who might have an interest in the group's activities.

I think that it's fair to say that if you are afraid of showing affection, you are afraid to be a leader. Leadership implies an ability to pull together one's emotional power and passion and to direct these qualities in such a way that the members of the group will respond. Your demonstration of affection will be evidence of the fact that the members of the group and yourself are capable of fulfilling a meaningful purpose, that without them you would be impotent of achievement.

4 / The first meeting

At your first meeting, you should feel as if you were entertaining a group of people in your home, welcoming them and making them feel comfortable. Make an effort to keep the names straight.

Greet each person as he or she arrives and exchange pleasantries. At a large meeting, this may not be possible, but at least you can greet those you know and introduce yourself to those whom you have not met.

If you have been named chairman of a committee consisting of persons you don't know, get as much information as possible about them before the meeting. Ask the person who appointed the committee members. You don't have to conduct an investigation, but it would be advisable to know of members' general backgrounds, interests, and training.

Occasionally one finds himself asked to serve as chairman of a committee, moderator of a panel, head of a commission, and so on, without knowing the agency or organization planning the meeting. At other times, you may be acquainted with the organization but unfamiliar with the program or project. In such instances, it would be helpful to contact the person responsible for the meeting and request additional information. They often may assume you are acquainted with their work when actually you are not.

Planning activities

If you are meeting with a group of children or adolescents for the first time, it would be helpful to plan on some definite activities for the first meeting. If it is an interest group, such as a craft class or recreation group, the type of activity is obvious. But if it is a new group—such as those established from time to time by churches, school, YMCAs and YWCAs—it is wise to plan projects that are not too complex or which would take too long to complete.

You may not have a lead on the interests of the members. In that case, it would be advisable to anticipate some of the natural interests of the age group. Games that are appropriate and easy to learn, craft projects, songs to sing around a campfire if the meeting is held outside, might be in order. But you should plan to be flexible and be prepared with more ideas than you will be able to use during the course of the meeting.

Arrive early

It is important for the leader to get to the meetings early, particularly the first one. You should allow sufficient time to be sure that everything is prepared for the members by the time they arrive. There can be problems—the lighting, seating arrangements, tables, blackboard, a slide projector that didn't show up, or a meeting in an adjoining room which would not be compatible with yours.

I had to learn my lesson the hard way on this score. On one occasion I had been instrumental in bringing together both youth and adult representatives of various organizations to discuss new recreation programs for the community. We had twice the attendance we expected and found ourselves in a room not half as large as we needed. I arrived later than I should have and the room was already overflowing. We finally gained permission to use a school auditorium but we had lost part of our evening and, needless to say, some of our crowd with the delay. It was poor planning on my part and the problem was further complicated by my not being early enough to see what was happening.

On another occasion I had been asked to serve as chairman of a special commission named by the governor on juvenile delinquency. I had planned to use some printed material at the opening of the meeting which I felt would be particularly useful to us in establishing our goals. The agency providing the material had promised to deliver it to our meeting room prior to the time we convened. I arrived at about the same time as the other members of the commission and discovered the material had not been delivered. It arrived about midway through our meeting and was not nearly as effective. If I had arrived early enough, I could have picked up the material myself.

If you are planning to use equipment such as movie or slide projectors, tape recorders, or whatever, it is best to see that this equipment is set up several hours in advance. You will then have ample opportunity to check out the equipment, to be sure that it is all there, to investigate electrical outlets, lighting, seating arrangements, and so forth. While it is necessary to be properly organized for all meetings, it can be particularly awkward at the first meeting when participants will get their first impressions of you as a leader. Some people can take things like the wrong room for the crowd, poor heating or air conditioning, failure of equipment to work properly in their stride and do not allow these things to affect their response to meetings. But others allow such matters to so upset them that they will leave or they will remain critical throughout the meeting.

Planning

On the day of your first meeting as leader, it will be best to keep going over things you should do and not do. Don't try to apply everything suggested the first time out. Just remember the business about poise and remaining calm. If you can remain relaxed, you will be amazed how many things will occur to you as you need them.

Try hard not to think about yourself. Think of the other people and make them feel welcome and comfortable. If they feel at ease, they will go a long way in making you feel at ease.

Above everything else, be yourself. Be the best leader that you can and be willing to learn from anyone you can, but don't try to copy other leaders. No two people function in the same way, so capitalize on your own strengths and talents. And whatever you do, do not approach your group with an apologetic attitude. Be confident and they will be confident of you. If you make a mistake, admit it, make amends if necessary, and move on. You wouldn't linger on other people's mistakes so give yourself the same break.

To a greater or lesser extent, your procedures for carrying on the meeting will depend upon the type of group you are leading. Procedures will be discussed in Chapters 11 and 12 for different types of organizations, commissions, and clubs. If a formal procedure is used in your group and you are not completely familiar with it, it might be wise to have an outline in hand. Even though you feel you are quite familiar with the procedures, you will find that at the time of the meeting you will be more relaxed if you don't have to worry about forgetting something.

Working together

Every meeting of the board of directors, a standing or special committee, an advisory council, an executive council, or a staff conference, brings forth differences in attitudes and points of view. Every club, service-giving agency, fraternal order, lodge, discussion group, encounter group, adult or youth organization discloses varying and what at times appears to be irreconcilable convictions. Such situations are bound to arise with every group effort at one time or another. When they do, there is a demand for the kind of leader who rises above mere chairmanship to bring out the process of integrated and creative group deliberation.

It is generally recognized today that most problems affecting people are too complex to be solved by the thinking of individuals in isolation, regardless of how intelligent and creative they may be. As a leader, you will realize that it is well nigh impossible for you to consider all of the facts necessary for a correct solution of problems, taking into account the differences of opinions between members of a group.

In most situations, people show a disposition to work together and they welcome the stimulation of other minds. They believe that through the pooling of ideas some better ideas and ways of doing business will evolve. In whatever field of human aspiration and endeavor we consider, we usually find this willingness to work together growing under the stress of modern living. People from all walks of life realize the need to work closely together for greater understanding, harmony, and the fulfillment of human capacities. The process of people coming together to share, communicate, and possibly reach decisions affecting themselves and others is perhaps the only successful way of fully grasping the nature of problems, identifying the issues involved, and bringing forth solutions acceptable to all.

It should not be imagined, however, that this process is automatic, that productivity will necessarily occur. The group process is largely dependent upon the leader's competent use of known techniques. Most group meetings are a coming together of a relatively small number of people, between eight and eighty and, again generally speaking, the smaller the group, the more effective will be the results of the meeting. In the final analysis, the purpose of all meetings is to foster understanding, to share, to create new ideas, and to reach agreement.

It is the experience of most leaders that the best meeting results occur when the leader has supervised all of the preparations prior to the meeting. Group meetings other than the membership type may involve a process of selecting persons with a special background or expertise to attend a hearing, forum, or discussion. Sometimes such meetings are open to the public or to certain specified groups. When the meeting does not involve a membership, is not open to the general public, and is not being held for a specific group, the question of selecting participants arises. This is usually determined by the nature and scope of the meeting or conference. A general principle which can be used is to try to gain representation from the various special interest groups who will be affected by the outcome of the meeting.

With the meeting to be held with selected persons, the first decision you must make as the leader is to determine the major reason for calling the group together. This in itself will determine largely whom you will invite and to what extent you will seek their active participation during the meeting.

You will want to plan carefully in advance an agenda of matters to be considered. If at all possible, this agenda should be supplied in advance to all participants. If you can develop good public relations with and between the participants, you will have taken a big step toward assuring that they will come to the meeting prepared to work out differences, reach understandings, develop new approaches, and come up with solutions to problems. This can be accomplished in a variety of ways. If you know the participants and they know each other, little spadework may be necessary, unless, of course, there are some strong differences of opinion or conflicts of interests. If this is the case, you may wish to visit with them individually or, perhaps, bring small groups together prior to the larger meeting. If you do not know the participants, personal contact would be in order. If this is not feasible, telephone calls can be useful and if this, too, is not possible, you will have to rely on your written correspondence. If the latter prevails, try to supply as much information as possible, and send along printed information materials when available. When controversy will be an obvious factor at the meeting, make every effort to resolve these differences during smaller conferences, luncheons, coffee conversations, or whatever prior to the general meeting. Use whatever time, energy, and public relations are accessible to assure your success in reaching desired goals before the meeting takes place.

As a leader you will be anxious to discover what people mean as contrasted with what they say and the way they say it. It is important that the discussions transcend mere debate and you will want to discourage gestures on the part of the participants to argue for argument's sake.

Problems of communication

It is advisable to bear in mind that there are multiple meanings conveyed in the communications between people. What people say is by no means all that they are imparting in their speech. Language, as a matter of fact, may be the least important thing. There is first the meaning which language is endeavoring to convey. Then, there is the speaker's feeling or attitude about what he is saying. Further, the tone in which something is said implies the speaker's attitude toward those to whom he is speaking. Finally, there is the ultimate effect which the speaker is trying to convey with words, gestures, and feelings. Remember that there are the conscious meanings of the speaker and unconscious ones which, nevertheless, may come through in his speech.

The more we examine the problems related to communication, the more we realize how really complicated it can be. For not only are there the problems of the speaker endeavoring to convey what he means but, on the other end, there are the listeners who will add their own meaning to his words, interpret from their own experiences the significance of his gestures, and inject their own feelings and attitudes into the final translation.

One preliminary factor frequently overlooked that probably causes more confusion and produces more disappointing results than any other has to do with not letting the participants know what is expected of them and not making it explicitly understood what the limits of their authority are. The membership of organizations and groups which meet fairly regularly will more likely understand the extent of their authority. But even within such groups, ad hoc committees are sometimes named which do not fully understand their roles and relationship toward the organization. All of this should be made clear in the beginning, that is, at the time or soon after the committee or subcommittee is established. When a special group or committee is meeting only once or for a short series, the failure of the members clearly to understand the extent of authority can be disastrous. Whether an established, on-going organization or a group called together for a temporary purpose, there is no better time than the first meeting for the leader to spell out the purpose and goals of the organization or group, its authority, and the relationship of subgroups to the total group. If time does not allow for this matter to be presented sufficiently at the first meeting, it would be well for you, as leader, to see that guidelines are drafted and copies given to all members or participants.

Many heartaches and hurt feelings can be avoided if the leader makes certain that all assignments are clearly understood. I recall one special committee in which all the members serving were disappointed, and one had sufficiently damaged feelings to drop out of the organization. Several of us were assigned by the president of that organization to make recommendations for legislative reforms in statutes pertaining to correctional schools. We thought our committee fully understood the stand of the organization on these matters and that we were merely to present these ideas to sympathetic legislators. Our report was referred to an interested state senator who promised to submit a bill. When the bill was presented in the state senate, the president of our organization became upset, stating that the recommendations were to have been reviewed by the organization's executive committee prior to being presented to the legislature. Members of our special committee were highly irritated by this and voted to disband the committee, with the chairman stating, "If he (the president) wants to handle the matter like that, let him handle the whole thing!"

The process of persons coming together to consider issues can have several results. If the meeting is of an informational nature, the participants may be able to offer special information. An advisory meeting will result in the participants assenting or acquiescing. If the meeting is held for the purpose of negotiating something, participants may give their consent or they may compromise. Certainly compromise is common enough but one should bear in mind that it usually leaves much to be desired. No particular interest in the group has been completely satisfied. The participants accept the outcome but with enough reservations that probably will require future adjustments.

Another outcome can be an agreement on a new combination of ideas. This creative process takes into account the ideas of the participants and improves upon them. While the leader may not be the one who formulates the new combination, the success of the meeting may largely depend upon his ingenuity in capitalizing on such presentations and gaining closure on them.

If not predetermined by the nature of the organization or precedent established by earlier meetings, it will be necessary for you, as the leader, to decide what method you will apply in conducting the discussion part of the meeting.

You can rely on the method of asking questions. It will not necessarily be required of you, as the leader, to make statements. You can direct the questions to other members of the group. The method is a mixture of questions and answers directed and moderated by the leader. With this method, the leader usually decides in advance what the solution of the problem is and then he guides the participants with skillful maneuvers until he reaches the desired conclusion. A third method is generally considered the soundest method by which genuine agreement is reached by a group. The problem is fully stated by the leader or a designated representative and then all divergent experiences and opinions related to it are explored by the participants. With this method, the leader guides the discussion but only to the extent of allowing all participants to have their say, and he stands prepared to abide by the conclusions reached.

It might be helpful to ask yourself the following questions as you proceed with such a meeting:

1. Have I stated the problems accurately and completely, bringing out all of the facts?

2. Have I entertained an adequate range of questions in order to bring out various points of view?

3. Have I clarified meanings and required others to do so?

4. Have I helped the participants see the difference between real conflicts of opinion and simple misunderstandings?

5. Have we managed to keep our perspectives about major and minor differences and tried to dispose of them so that we can clear the way for others?

6. Have I managed to keep the attention focused on the issues?

7. Have I kept the tone of the meeting friendly and yet objective?

8. Have I summarized from time to time and directed the discussions toward solutions?

9. Have I diplomatically been able to terminate discussion on an issue when I have sensed that we have reached a formula for solution?

Try to discover the deeper, sometimes hidden, reasons behind superficially stated differences. You should try to prevent arguments from developing over small technical details which may distract from the principal considerations.

There is always the temptation to cut through and save time by providing a better answer. Factually, this may be the case but your real job as a leader is to help the members do their own best thinking and they will feel a much greater sense of accomplishment if you assist them in this. That is not to say, however, that you should allow them to deceive themselves by coming up with vague and pretentious formulas.

People's feelings and opinions are precious and fragile; treat them kindly regardless of how foolish or irrelevant their comments are. But get solid evidence in the most efficient manner possible. Seek the advice of an informed speaker or panel of experts. If there are appropriate books, films, tapes, pamphlets, use them to inform the group.

Where a considerable amount of emotion exists within the group, don't avoid letting members honestly release their feelings. Disagreements can be handled in such a way as to draw the group closer together rather than dividing it.

Occasionally you will discover that a member is totally committed to an opinion or idea and refuses to compromise. The wise leader will point out that this person evidently believes that this is a position he must take and that his minority opinion is respected. This lets him know that he is accepted even though the group may vote otherwise.

Now and then, even in the friendliest of groups, an outburst of anger can occur. When it does, immediately take over the meeting, summarize what has been said up to that point and draw the replies to yourself.

Timing

While some organized groups have a specified length of time for their meetings, many others do not. Many meetings have a tendency to drag on too long, and then unsuccessful efforts are made to reach agreements, complete discussions, all in the last five minutes. As leader, you should plan the meeting in order that items on the agenda are completed within a certain time period. A good idea is to have several time checks along the way. Although it is difficult to generalize on the length of time for all kinds of meetings, few should ever last longer than two hours. If, as in the case of some seminars and workshops, the meeting is scheduled for all morning or all afternoon, you should provide time for a coffee break or at least a recess period. Even when a break is not scheduled, it might be wise to call one when you notice participants getting tired or their attention beginning to wander.

There will be times when deep emotions are involved and when considerable tension is apparent. Then it would be wise to suggest a moment of pause, of complete silence in the deliberations. This allows each participant to evaluate the situation for himself. It gives each person the chance to withdraw from the anxiety of those heated moments and tension is reduced. As Socrates paused in his deliberations, waiting for the promptings of the "demon" within, he was not being superstitious, but he was borrowing a little time in which to think reasonably and draw matters into perspective.

Do not hesitate to introduce a pause in the deliberations. Do not apologize for this suggestion but announce it as a normal and natural step. Explain that you expected this moment to arrive, that it is welcome, and that this is what is best to do at such times. I have noticed that groups which fail to take advantage of a few moments of pause in the discussions to relieve sustained concentration—and unfortunately most groups do—lose the best fruits of discussion: reflective judgment.

Finally, with nearly all meetings there is the question as to the precise method for registering the decisions of the group. With certain organized groups, boards of directors, formal conferences, voting may be required. When this is not the case, however, there is a great deal to be said for allowing participants to summarize. When none volunteer, you can sometimes stimulate them by asking questions by way of your own summary. The members are then involved in the meeting—or at least invited to be—to the very end.

5 / Creating atmosphere

Attitude

Your attitude as a leader is all-important in creating an atmosphere in which thegroup memberseel free to express themseles. Problem-slving is much ore effective in such climate. Participants will be more likely to develop their potentiality when a relaxed and friendly climate prevails.

It is nearly impossible to overemphasize the importance of your friendly and relaxed attitude as a leader, and it is helpful to remember that the outward expression reflects the inner feelings.

We have to be willing to allow for differences in leaders, of course. Some people are just naturally careless about physical arrangements. They may be friendly, outgoing persons who care a great deal about the feelings of others. They may be excellent leaders but neglect details. Another leader might be very particular about room arrangements, well-organized, and a stickler for details but finds it difficult to relate to people. Therefore, again, it is difficult to set up absolute standards. Yet it is safe to say that a clean, well-organized meeting room reflects more favorably on the leader than

46

a room which is a mess at meeting time. If you are the kind of person who is likely to overlook the importance of the condition of the meeting room, it might be well to appoint a committee or ask others to handle the physical arrangements.

Seating arrangements are important because they affect the degree of communication between the participants. A room arranged like a classroom forces the participants to look at the backs of heads instead of faces. Communication depends not only on the voice, but also on facial expressions, gestures, and other clues. Your group may be too large to do other than a classroom arrangement, but to the extent possible, try to arrange the group in a circular fashion so that the members can at least partially face each other.

If your group is an informal one and you are holding a series of meetings within a short period of time, you might wish to experiment with seating arrangements to let the participants experience differences. You could start out with conventional seating arrangements and then change the seats to a circle. The members will probably be amazed at the difference in communication and their enthusiasm will show a dramatic change. Ideally, the seating arrangement for maximum communication is one in which no one person is outside of the leader's vision and, preferably, not outside the vision of any other member of the group.

Names

Social climateis of great importance in encouraging response and participation from group members. People communicate much better with one another if they know each other's names. It is particularly important for the leader to know the names of the participants. His use of a person's name provides the means whereby others can learn. Names printed in large type on lapel cards or place cards, if tables are used, can be very helpful.

There are numerous methods for learning names. Dr. Frank Cheavens, a consultant to various organizations and foundations on group work, suggests that if the members of the group will be meeting together for a time, you separate the group into pairs at the first meeting. In each couple, individuals learn one another's names and something of his or her background. The leader should then go around the circle, asking each person to introduce his or her partner and offer a brief biographical sketch. Dr. Cheavens feels that the time used in this exercise is well spent and that the participants will feel they know each other much better than if there is simply some kind of roll call or introductions by themselves.

After the first exercise in becoming acquainted, it can be helpful to ask the participants to identify themselves before they make comments or direct questions to the leader. The exercise can be abandoned later.

It might appear that too great an emphasis is being given to names, but if you will stop and analyze various social situations, I think you will agree that a person is more likely to communicate with someone whose name he knows.

The period preceding a meeting can be productive if the leader sees to it that persons are introduced as they arrive. No one should be overlooked. The leader should introduce himself and in turn introduce the individual to others. At large gatherings where many persons are coming into the room or hall at a time, personal introductions, of course, are not possible.

When a group member is late in a small, informal meeting, the leader should interrupt the discussions or proceedings to welcome this person. As the leader, you may wish to say something like, "We're happy you made it, Mrs. Jones. We were just talking about . . ." and you can bring the late arrival up-to-date on what has taken place.

Your constant efforts to be conscious of everyone and to make each feel as if he belonged will go a long way in building rapport. Most people attending meetings experience a mild feeling of being threatened. What you do as a leader can help diminish these feelings and make the participants feel as though they belong.

One of the big reasons people join groups is to belong and to meet people with whom they share common interests. And what most people want from a leader above everything is personal concern and involvement. The leader's attitude about what happens to the members will add an important quality to the atmosphere of a meeting. In our society, too many people pride themselves on their indifference. More than likely their gestures of not caring are really expressions of fear. They are afraid to commit themselves to life and to other people. But I have never known a successful leaer who was unwilling to risk his personal commitment in order to give life a real meaning.

"Play life cool and you may freeze," Norman Vincent Peale has stated. "Play it hot and, even if you get burned, you will at least shed warmth over the world."

Jack London, the novelist, once stated, "I would rather be ashes than dust. I would rather that my spark would burn out in a brilliant blaze than be stifled by dry rot."

There may be times when you, as a leader, feel anything but enthusiastic. But you will have to rise to the occasion if the atmosphere of the meeting is going to be a positive one. Here we can call upon the words of psychologist William James who stated, "If you want a quality, act as if you already had it." The principle works with enthusiasm just as it does with despondency.

When things seem to have gone stale, ask yourself how some other leader would have handled your tasks. What imaginative measures would he have taken to freshen the scene? In his book, Enthusiasm Makes the Difference, Norman Vincent Peale tells of a sales manager for a wholesale grocery store who accepted the notion that nothing could be sold in a section of his city. He got this notion from his predecessor. Then management brought in a new man who was not aware of this so-called arid spot in his territory. He approached the job with energy and enthusiasm and soon made impressive sales. In a very short time, he reported to the home office that he had come upon virgin terrltory and was moving in on it.

Getting along with people

One of the blessings of being human is that we can learn from our mistakes. Our failures show us what not to do. Our successes, on the other hand, can open doors to even greater success. When we do something well, we try to repeat it, and this search for new techniques can make any task worth experiencing.

Most people probably fail at the leadership role because they haven't developed techniques, or talents, for getting along with all kinds of people. Graduate psychology students at Harvard University carried out a study in 1969 of 4000 persons in various trades and professions who had been discharged from their jobs in the Boston area. The study was conducted, in cooperation with the U.S. Department of Labor, for the purpose of determining the psychological reasons why people are fired. It was learned that about one-third had lost their jobs because they lacked skill or otherwise could not do the job. But the other two-thirds lost their jobs because they conflicted with their fellow workers.

Having a good personal relationship with people is by far the most important factor for the leader to be able to create a warm, friendly, and exciting atmosphere at group meetings.

People are just about the same everywhere. It is no more difficult to adjust satisfactorily to them in one place than in another. The first requirement is to learn to get along with oneself. The art of getting along with others imposes some very personal obligations. For one thing, we cannot afford to lose our tempers, for when we do, we've lost control of ourselves. We will always be suspect in people's eyes afterwards, and they will always wonder if they can trust us. No one, actually, can afford the habit of being a gossip and a leader, least of all. People may listen to but will have little respect for anyone who talks about others. Buck-passing is another behavior which most certainly does not belong in the leader's bag.

A wise philosopher once said, "The only safe way to destroy an enemy is make him your friend." If you discover members of your group who, for one reason or another, seem opposed to you, try your skill in converting them. In any case, the process will help you to see some of your own faults, and this is one of the best ways to get others to like you.

Certainly one of the most important factors in getting along with others is learning to think about them first instead of yourself. It is amazing how well people will respond to you if they discover that you are genuinely interested in them. They find security in the fact that you know them, call them by name, appreciate their interests, and have a regard for their welfare.

Psychologists are quick to point out that the deepest urge of human nature is the desire to be important. What a miracle you can achieve, then, by giving people this feeling of importance through your appreciation of them. If you can satisfy this hunger in people, you will have found the key to successful leadership.

Perhaps it will help to remember that every man or woman or youth in your group will feel superior to you in some way, and you will win their hearts if you recognize their talents and importance. Flattery will not do, however. You have to seek out people's qualities and interests and show honest appreciation.

Dale Carnegie once stated, "If you want to make friends, forget yourself. People are not interested in you. They are interested in themselves. That is why you can make more friends in two months by becoming interested in other people than you can in two years by trying to get other people interested in you."

One of the gravest faults of many leaders is to dominate discussions. They need to talk less and listen more. If we encourage others to express their views, to tell us how they feel, they will love us for it and will leave meetings feeling satisfied and with a sense of achievement. Real listening—so dependent upon our genuine interest in people—is one of the highest compliments we can pay to others. They will not forget and will more than likely support us in our leadership role.

As a leader, it will be necessary for you to be able to take criticism gracefully, whether or not it is justified. When you accept the role of leader, you have placed yourself in the path of criticism; it is part of the game. Former president Harry S. Truman put it rather well when he stated, "If you can't stand the heat, stay out of the kitchen."

Sir John Simon, British Chancellor of the Exchecquer, kept a constant reminder of this in the form of a tapestry which hung on his office wall and read, "To Escape Criticism, Say Nothing, Do Nothing, Be Nothing."

The higher you climb, the more you do, the more original and creative you are, the more you will become a target of criticism. You should expect it, prepare for it, but do not go out of your way to invite it. You delude yourself if you believe that as long as you make an effort to do the right thing, you will please everyone. You won't. A means of providing universal satisfaction has yet to be discovered.

But while you do not seek out criticism, you can accept it as a contribution to your life. Instead of resenting criticism, use it to learn what you can about yourself and about others. When you discover you are in the wrong, admit it quickly. Make no effort to defend yourself. Your willingness to criticize yourself usually turns your would-be critics into your defenders.

In order to benefit from criticism, you must learn to be objective. You can control its effect on you so that you can remain composed. If you become unduly concerned about the reactions or opinions of others, you will lose your poise and this hinders your creativity. Learn to accept the criticism, measure it objectively, keep your perspective, and make up your own mind. People will respect your honesty.

I have seen good leaders lose confidence and a perspective of their self-worth in the presence of persons of great wealth. It was as though they accepted the degree of wealth as the true measure of success and, therefore, they felt inferior in the presence of the well-to-do. The person who becomes inhibited in the presence of the rich seems to be paying homage to the belief that such people dominate all situations and people. Rather than make this mistake, respect such persons for their talent of making money but at the same time acknowledge that these persons may be inferior to you in many other ways. Are their husbands or wives or children happy, self-fulfilling individuals? Do they make personal—besides money—contributions to the community? Do they have many real friends? Will they be remembered for their warmth and kindnesses? Are they talented musicians, artists, writers, actors, baseball players? Perhaps they are all of these things. Wonderful. I am not suggesting that you try to find fault—as many envious people do—with these persons. Give all the credit that's due and don't lose your own sense of values. Wealth is only one way of measuring a person's success; it may be the least important one. If having money is a quality of the self, it certainly is a most transient one.

But if lasting success is not found in the accumulation of wealth, how can it be achieved? Those whose achievements have lasted and whom history has finally called "great" are not the predators and the accumulators, but the self-giving: Gandhi, who gave himself to the freedom of man; Albert Schweitzer, who gave himself to the needy and oppressed; Kennedy, who gave himself for the country; Beethoven, who gave the world a greater music; Florence Nightingale, who gave herself to nursing; Shakespeare, who gave us a grander literature; Bruno, who gave himself that the truth might live. The really successful are always the givers.

There is no greater barrier to your success as a leader than to allow yourself to be inhibited or intimidated by members of the group. There may be members of the group who would make better leaders than you. But you are the best leader at this moment in time and if they didn't believe this, they wouldn't have chosen you to lead. You are you, with your own strengths, weaknesses, and talents. The members expect you to put your skills to work for them; would you ask less of yourself? When we talk about atmosphere, we can include the place where the meeting is held, room arrangements, decorations, lighting, sounds or their absence, program agenda, etc. But the lion's share of the atmosphere is going to be created by the manner in which you function as leader. So be yourself, your real self. That's the person the members elected or appointed and that's the leader they want.

6 / Establishing goals

You will be doing your job as a leader when the members of your group are working together toward a goal which they believe is desirable.

What kinds of goals do the members desire? What kinds of goals appeal to the members of your particular group? In what way are the goals of organized groups determined, maintained, shared, altered? How do you as a leader know that your goals are attractive? How are you able to determine this?

Different goals

Bear in mind that there may be different sets of goals that will determine the framework within which you must function. You will have your own goals; these bear the stamp of your philosophy of life, and one of the reasons, certainly, why you have accepted the leadership of the group in the first place. The sponsoring agency, institution, foundation, whatever, also has its purpose, reason for existence, and it has established policies and procedures within which it expects its leader or leaders to operate. Then the group itself and the individual members have their goals.

Goals may be different but they are not necessarily in conflict with each other. However, there are bound to be times when the goals of the members may come into conflict with policies of the agency. A local chapter may disagree with the decisions of the parent organization. Your task as a leader is to develop the best possible interrelationship between the members and the group, between the group and the parent organization when there is one, and between the group and the community.

Within the context of these various restrictions, the leader must have sound objectives for goal realization. One of the primary duties of the leader is to make a critical study of objectives. This is particularly true in those organizations that provide some service to the community or state.

There are short-range and long-range objectives. A Scout troop may decide to hold a weekend camp-out. This is a short-term goal. The long-range goal is to help boys grow into responsible manhood. The League of Women Voters may plan a study on the probate court. This is a short-term goal, whereas the organization's long-term goal is to help people to become more knowledgeable citizens.

A goal can be defined as the direction of effort of an associated group of people. But it is of some help to distinguish between primary and secondary goals, i.e., between basic and supplementary objectives.

A commission might be appointed by a mayor to study the need for youth recreation centers within the city. In the course of their investigation, the commission learns that an increase in juvenile vandalism and alcohol and drug addition corresponds to a decrease in the use of youth recreation centers and various activity programs. They determine that the construction of new centers and remodeling of existing ones will necessitate an increase in taxes. But they are businessmen opposed to an increase in city taxes. They face a dilemma as to primary objectives, a conflict between their business interests and the honest fulfillment of the commission's assignment. If they act with integrity, of course, they will file an honest report with the mayor, and will need to place their business interests at this time in a supplementary position.

The point is that a group, and particularly its leader, must be prepared to distinguish between those goals which are basic and those goals which carry a lesser importance. The inability to discriminate between basic and supplementary objectives can be very threatening to one's effectiveness as a leader.

Establishing priorities

On few occasions does one objective alone determine action. Usually there is a need for the balancing of factors among a number of objectives. From a practical standpoint, your job as a leader is to bring the various factors into sufficient balance as a whole in order to be acceptable to the members. Generally, supplementary objectives can be realized if they are part of, and at least, are not in conflict with the primary objectives. Better still, of course, if the supplementary goals complement the primary ones.

The objectives of organized human effort are as varied as human needs and interests. People are attracted to these endeavors because they provide outlets for activities that satisfy certain facets of human nature.

Objectives are more attractive when the pursuit of them helps people to attain something they desire—fun, social contacts, professional status, growth, education, business and professional contacts, recreational activities, community service. From the individual's standpoint, goals are worthwhile when they enhance his or her sense of self-achievement. Regardless of how willing a follower may be to give himself over to the leader and his cause, sooner or later the intelligent person comes to realize that one who loses himself may eventually find himself. The amazing paradox of selflessness developing greater selfhood is a profound truth one should bear in mind in understanding and developing the relation of leader to follower.

The demand upon you as a leader is to recognize the various qualities of the individual and to be aware of the characteristics of human nature. The basic principles of leadership require a knowledge of human behavior, basic and refined desires, dreams and aspirations, and the conditions and situations which confer fulfillment and contentment. Some of this knowledge you have gained from experience, some has been provided by your intuition, and some you will gain from study.

Individual needs

Within each of us there are a number of interests which we endeavor to fulfill in our own way. Most of these desires we share in common with other human beings, but there are also ingredients which set us apart as individuals. Intelligence, temperament, talents, creative powers, strengths and weaknesses vary from person to person. Because of the unique, individual characteristics of human nature, an understanding of how individuals reach self-actualization is necessary for one's own self-discovery. As a leader, one cannot afford to lose sight of the individual's need for self-realization. In the final analysis, the individual follows a leader only so long as he believes that the meaning of his own life is being enhanced.

While all of this may seem rather obvious, it is amazing how few organizational situations there are in our modern society where the option of individual choice is offered. Not only in business situations but also in fraternal, religious, and educational groups people participate without having a say in the formulation of goals and with no greater affirmation of these goals than the mere act of joining. And they join because they believe their membership will benefit them in some way. Yet, the most intelligent, ambitious, creative, and searching individuals will sooner or later gravitate only toward those groups in which they can play more active roles.

In my early experience of teaching a Sunday school class, I experienced some problems with an aggressive and disruptive thirteen-year-old youngster. I finally talked with the minister of the church about him and was told, "Try to channel his energy, but don't turn it off. That kid needs every outlet we can supply. He needs to express himself, and, in a sense, get some things off his chest. His parents don't have time for him, and I'm told he has few friends. But here he feels that he belongs, that this is one place he can be somebody."

The minister must have been right, for the church continued to be an important place to Dave. Today he is minister of a large church in Dallas.

Some of the least ambitious workers in large factories may be regular whirlwinds at their lodges, service clubs, or at home working on their cars, building cabinets, or taking care of their lawns. Away from the job, they feel like they have a vote, a chance to make decisions, to change things.

The kinds of objectives that are attractive to people should be known by leaders. The objectives which the members of a group will follow and the leader they will serve will largely depend on the leader's ability to develop and maintain their egos and promote their growth.

The individual may not understand his own inner desires and needs and one of the leader's tasks is to help in this discovery. It is an observant leader who can make others aware of needs and aspirations in themselves of which they were not previously aware. This happens somewhat frequently but in the end the experience only has real and lasting meaning if the individual discovers a value in the process. In order for a goal to be truly attractive, an individual must be able to identify with it.

In your service as a leader it would be well now and then to ask yourself—and to ask the members of your group if not directly, then by forming the question in your gestures—if the objectives of the organization are of such a nature that the members can experience enthusiasm when striving for them?

There may be some difference in the definition of goals and objectives as set forth in the organization's by-laws or by yourself in public speeches, and the way they are defined in action by committee chairmen or by yourself, for that matter, in your regular contacts with the members. It is necessary to recognize that objectives are valuable only to the extent that the members can share in fulfilling them.

Creating objectives

In fulfilling objectives, the leader's role has two aspects. On one side, the leader is the representative or the symbolized embodiment of predetermined goals, and to this extent he does not actually create the objectives. Rather, he puts these objectives into action. On the other hand, the leader does play a significant role in creating new and perhaps greater objectives. If leaders did not perform these creative tasks, organizations would grow stagnant and die, as alas, some do when their leader fails to exercise sufficient vision.

In order to illustrate the first type of leader, let us imagine that a group of citizens who meet regularly for coffee each morning fall into a discussion about the need for a community theater in their town. Several of the participants are sufficiently excited about the idea that they accept Mr. Smith's suggestion that they gather at his home on a certain evening to discuss the matter. At the meeting in his home, Mr. Smith more or less serves as informal chairman. The group concludes that they are interested enough to test the idea of establishing a community theater with other interested persons. They ask Mr. Smith to serve as acting chairman, to locate a site for the meeting, and to make arrangements for public notice of the meeting. When the meeting is held, Mr. Smith makes some preliminary remarks, states the general objective, and moderates the discussion which follows. The meeting is concluded with plans to hold additional meetings and Mr. Smith is elected chairman. He is now the leader of the community theater group.

In this case, the objective has grown out of the interest of the group. It has been stated and the membership is formed of persons already interested in this objective. The leader's role, then, is to work with the group in order to give form to the stated objective.

To illustrate the second type of leadership, imagine that a steering committee of the political party not in office is preparing to launch a campaign for governor. After considerable discussion, it is decided that in order to win the election, an issue of considerable importance will need to be brought to the attention of the voters. While in one sense, the greater objective is known—to get the party in office—the underlying objective is somehow to focus attention on matters of real concern to the public in such a way as to offer new and appealing solutions.

At this point Mr. Carter, an attorney and a state senator, emerges

as a leader by presenting some intelligent and well-articulated concepts for the party platform which are sufficiently different to be
creative, and yet familiar enough in scope and temper as to be
sympathetically received by the voters. As the new party leader, Mr.
Carter has, within the limits of the party, the opportunity to create
objectives.

Not infrequently a citizen of the community will enlist public
supporters by protesting that the taxpayers are not being sufficiently
consulted as to zoning laws or on matters regarding the public school
system. Although his motive may be to sell some real estate at a
greater profit or to improve the school building attended by his own
children, nevertheless, when his proposals carry public appeal, he
has emerged as a leader by offering new or broader objectives.

The ability to arouse support for a cause is important to a leader.
The process can be a crucial one at times, particularly if the aim is
not a popular one. If, for example, a local mental health association's
status and accepted importance in the community is dependent upon
the organization's ability and willingness to establish an around-
the-clock emergency telephone service and the only way this is
possible is through the voluntary help of the members, the talents of
the leader may well be tested. Can he make the members realize the
importance of providing this service for the community? Will they be
convinced that the only possible way is by volunteer efforts? Do they
trust him sufficiently to accept his evaluation of the matter? And can
he persuade the members to accept the challenge with feelings of
pride and personal achievement?

It is well to remember that to a large extent the acceptance of
objectives depends on the degree that people can discover a direct
contribution to their own lives. I am not saying that people are only
selfish and egocentric, but I am saying that any efforts they make
must be translated and found to have meaning within the context of
their lives.

As a leader, you must not lose sight of the fact that the goals and
objectives of your organization can only be met when you have the
support of your members, and that this support is dependent upon
your ability to interpret objectives in such a manner so as to reveal

your interest in the welfare of the members. Your presentation of objectives requires complete candor and your arguments must be supported by the facts. If the members have faith in your integrity and believe that your suggestions bear the stamp of objective research, they will stand squarely behind you. While they may disagree with your findings and conclusions—you would not want it otherwise—they will not question your leadership.

If you are a creative leader, you will explore new possibilities for your organization. The ideas you will gather will come from your own experiences and insights gleaned from others. But the acceptance of these ideas can only be made by the members. Hopefully, you have made them feel a kinship with these ideas. To what extent the members feel that the ideas belong to them will depend upon the methods you use to acquaint them with the objectives. No special problem is involved when the group simultaneously discovers a common need or interest. This was the case with the community theater group mentioned earlier. Nor is there any particular problem when the members have been involved in developing current goals. But difficulties can arise in such organizations as the PTA which many parents join simply because their children attend elementary school. Problems occur when the leader fails to interpret adequately existing objectives and to make the new members feel that they will have the opportunity to share in the modification of the goals or to establish new ones. If the members do not experience this sense of belonging, chances are they will find little reason to support the organization's goals. Not having a voice in matters, they will feel used and such emotions foster resistance.

Sharing decision-making

It is necessary for the leader to inform the members and to give them the kind of experiences that will make them realize that their membership in, and contributions to, the organization are also good for them as individuals. Few groups can operate long merely through blind faith in the leader. While blind faith in the leader may occur with backward people, it seldom or ever happens with intelligent, educated people. The members of most groups in our society expect to share with the leader in the decision-making process.

We have all had experiences with institutions that acted as though mere existence was reason enough for being. The organization operates as an end in itself. Fitting into this classification are many foundations, agencies, churches, government bureaus, educational institutions, and so forth. When leaders merely go through the motions, doing what has always been done to fill the position and repeating the objectives of other days, then these goals will cease to elicit any excitement in the members, or the community for that matter. This living death is much less likely to happen in those organizations where all members have a voice in the selection and development of the goals and objectives of the organization.

In recent years, we have witnessed on college campuses some stimulating, if not always constructive, efforts on the part of the student body to modify antiquated and stereotyped administrative principles, curriculum, and methods of instructions. Reports of contributions made by well-organized student committees in which new life and purposes were injected into the institutions are not uncommon. There has been, of course, much irresponsible behavior on the part of some university students. This is unfortunate because it handicaps the serious efforts of students. However, the violence and the rebellion illustrate very well what can happen to an institution when real leadership deteriorates. And the moral of the story is that "revolution" does not exist when the members of a group, large or small, believe they have a voice in determining the objectives which affect their lives.

There have been many great leaders whose vision carried them beyond the understanding and the reach of their followers. The issues with which some of these leaders struggled—Christ, Socrates, Gandhi, Lincoln—were of such a magnitude that they had to go on regardless of how unpopular their stands with the multitudes. They *knew* they were right and they could allow nothing else to matter.

Yet, in the everyday affairs of men, the leader of a group accomplishes more of his objectives by using his persuasive influence. People will support your leadership if they believe that the goals you offer are the ones they prefer to seek. You can accurately assess the reception of your objectives if you are reasonably certain that the members of your group find them enriching to their lives.

In the final analysis, then, leadership is not a matter of clever maneuvering, manipulation, hypnosis, or salesmanship. Rather it is a matter of drawing forth from others those efforts, aspirations, and motives which are a true representation of their best inner selves. It is the business of helping people to discover that, in working with others toward a common goal, their individual wisdom, strength, and accomplishments are heightened and multiplied.

7 / Order, control, and discipline

There is a great deal of misunderstanding regarding the use of order and discipline while leading groups. Considerable attention has been focused in recent years on the free expression of thought, the avoidance of structure and boundaries that inhibit individualism and the democratic process.

Maintaining balance

As group leaders, we are oftentimes intimidated by members of a group who insist on expressing themselves whenever they are so inclined. They may be children or adults who have never learned the virtues of discipline and control, and they may be sufficiently self-centered to be oblivious to other persons' feelings and thoughts. On the other hand, they may not understand the individual's relationship to the group or the purpose to be served by teamwork within the organization. While it may not be your role to educate the members of your group in human relationships, your success as a leader and the success of the group as a whole will depend to a large extent upon your ability to protect the rights of each and every member, and provide to all equal opportunity for participation. As some members will be aggressive and others passive, it is your task to see that balance and harmony are maintained.

Joe M. was selected as chairman of a United Fund evaluation team. The task was for the group to meet on several consecutive evenings to consider the proposed budgets for a number of community organizations financed by the United Fund. Although familiar with the work of these agencies, Joe felt intimidated by two aggressive and well-known businessmen who dominated the first evening's proceedings. They did most of the talking and hardly gave the other eight members the opportunity to express their opinions. Before the group met the following evening, Joe had visited with a more experienced group leader who suggested that Joe try an around-the-table approach, whereby each member in turn is asked to express an opinion. Joe found this to be more successful.

There is no foolproof method, however, to balance group discussion. This is one of the greatest challenges faced by the group leader: balanced group participation. But some people are just more aggressive and verbal than others and are going to be more active regardless of anything the leader does. Since people function in different ways, it is impossible to force a balance between them. The best that you can hope for is to moderate the participation of the aggressive to the extent that it allows the more passive an opportunity to speak. Even taking turns cannot always balance, the few strong words of some and long dissertations by others. Sometimes the simple matter of looking beyond one member to another as though asking for an answer from this person will work. Sometimes you can carefully interrupt a long-winded speaker by making a quick comment on some point and then instead of returning the discussion to the first speaker say to another, "What do you think about this, Jim?" More likely than not, the members of the group will get the message and will monitor themselves. The leader should continue to work for this balance until it is in some degree achieved. If too great an insistence on this equilibrium is made by the leader in the beginning, however, the aggressive may be led to believe their participation is not appreciated and the passive will be forced to participate in ways unnatural to them. As all people do not march to the same drummer, their differences must be considered by the leader. His task is to put his group at ease, make them feel comfortable, and seek their participation without forcing it.

Importance of order

When you are serving as a leader of a group of children or young people, one of your tasks will be to help each individual to learn to control his behavior and to help the group as a whole to learn to take responsibility for managing their affairs. But you should be careful that you don't make the group dependent upon your controls. Rather, you should provide experiences through which the individual and the group can develop a degree of self-discipline. As the leader, you have to step in when a few members are spoiling the fun of the others. A certain amount of order must be maintained for the group to carry out its program.

The need for order does not mean that members march into the room, sit passively, and fold their hands. Members must feel free to express themselves. You should expect a lot of horseplay with any group that feels comfortable. But freedom does not imply chaos or a disregard for others. Nor does it imply such disorder that a meeting, program, or project can't proceed in orderly fashion.

While you will be striving toward helping the group establish its own controls, there will be occasions when the leader will have to set limitations. For the most part, these are largely determined by the policies and rules of the sponsoring organization, and the leader's impression of how well the group is functioning. It is your job to interpret any limitations on the group and help the members function comfortably within them.

Limitations should be kept to the minimum for any group. None should be established which are irrelevant to the group's goals and activities. Whether the group consists of young people, adults, or a mixture of both, limitations or rules which do not apply and do not make a contribution to the functioning of the group can only serve to inhibit it.

Planning

Problems can oftentimes be avoided if you will exercise imagination while preparing for a meeting. In addition to carefully going over the program agenda, you should give some thought to the physical facilities to be used. If the meeting is to be held indoors, will the temperature be comfortable? What other activities are being held in the building at the same time and how, if at all, will this affect the meeting? If the meeting is to be held outdoors, what provisions have been made for bad weather? What other activities will be held in the area? Indoors or outdoors, what about the available space? Is it adequate, or too great a space to be controllable? It will help if you can visualize the space through the eyes of the group members and foresee how they will utilize the space. These factors can have a considerable bearing on the order and control of the group.

If the meeting involves lively youngsters—whether they represent the membership or children of members—some thought needs to be given to hazards or to equipment which might be damaged. There may be a need to remove items, protect equipment, or even move to a different room. Aside from the possible physical dangers and threat to property, the presence and availability of interesting equipment distracts from the order of a meeting.

Mildred G. found it necessary to hold her children's art class, sponsored by the city's recreation commission, in a large workshop used by adult craft classes. All about were large power saws, lathes, and welding equipment. Mildred asked one of the craft members to attend her first meeting with the children. At the beginning of the meeting, this person explained to the children why the equipment was in the room and demonstrated the use of the equipment. Together they explained the dangers of the machinery and said that it was not to be touched at any time. At the same time, they explained the fun to be had in learning to use brushes and hand tools, and that when older they, too, would be able to use the power equipment. Their curiosity satisfied as to the functioning of the equipment, the children worked within their limitations.

Most of the time, you will have little difficulty in getting a meeting underway. If the members are unacquainted with one another, the start of the meeting can be a welcome relief from awkward attempts at conversation. On the other hand, if several members of the group are already acquainted, socially or professionally, it may prove difficult to disengage them from their premeeting discussion. Usually, however, a simple announcement—in a voice slightly louder than theirs—that it is time to get the meeting underway will turn the trick. If this fails, you may have to be divisive. One way is to select the speaker and say, "Excuse me, Frank, but do you know if so-and-so is coming to the meeting?" or whatever you can think of at the spur of the moment to ask him, and then while the conversation has been interrupted, announce that it is meeting time. One of the best procedures for getting the meeting rolling is to establish the practice of starting on time. If members expect this, they, too, will glance at their watches. Also it might be noted here that one of the strongest incentives to an orderly meeting, one that gets down to business and is devoid of extraneous discussions, is also to follow the practice of adjourning on time. The members know that if they keep their attention on the work at hand, they will get away on schedule. This will contribute to orderliness and their own self-discipline.

Children and other young people, however, are not usually as time-conscious as adults. Further, unless it is a group with which they have been meeting for some time, they are less likely to be acquainted with the purposes of the meeting. In such cases you will have to rely on a good program and something interesting at the start of the program to gain their attention. Failing that, you will have to be firm and establish limitations from the beginning. Again, the need for planning as to program and facilities becomes apparent.

It can be a truly upsetting experience for a leader when the group runs rampant. At such times, the leader must act quickly and decisively.

An inexperienced leader of a Boy Scout troop had to change plans for a camp-out because of rainy weather. The grounds of the regular campground were too muddy to use as a result of a flash downpour. One of the committee members suggested that the troop use the wooded area of his farm property where it had not rained. The troop leader accepted the offer without first checking out the property. When he and his troop arrived early in the evening, they discovered that the campgrounds were only a few yards from the farmer's livestock and tool buildings.

No sooner had the boys climbed from the cars than they were all over the farmer's property. Running in every direction, they climbed over the fences, into the haylofts, onto the tractors and other equipment, and tried to catch the calves, among other things. At first the leader stood perplexed in the middle of the barnyard, and it was of little help to his sense of inadequacy to have one of the older boys in the troop exclaim, "I don't think we should let them do that!"

Then the leader started yelling at the boys to come back. But nothing happened. The leader was disturbed because the boys ignored him, but he was also fearful that the boys might get hurt or damage the farmer's property.

Desperation finally moved him from his spot and he caught hold of one youngster as he was about to mount a garden tractor. A little angry by this time, he said firmly, "All right, that's about enough," and grabbed hold of the boy's arm. For a moment the boy tried to pull his arm away but when he saw how tightly it was being held, he climbed off the tractor. Several of the other boys, of course, were keeping one eye on the leader to see the outcome, and when the leader led the boy back to the car, several more followed. Soon they were reassembled by the cars where the leader laid down some rules as to boundaries for the campout. As a result of his firmness, the campout was carried out successfully without further incident. Needless to say, he might have saved himself some problems if he had checked out the site earlier in the day.

There is something wrong in the way a leader is handling a group of children if he constantly finds himself saying, "Don't do that." It would be well if he would spend some time visiting with more experienced leaders.

It is important that you maintain a friendly and warm attitude toward the members of the group, but you must be able to speak with assurance and firmness when a member is misbehaving. While it is humanly impossible not to become irritated and to show this annoyance once in a while, you must show you can control the group without resorting to anger. It is imperative in order to demand respect from the group that you can demonstrate you can control the situation without becoming emotionally upset.

Being consistent

Whether the group consists of children or adults, one of the most important qualities for a leader to cultivate is consistency. There is nothing more frustrating to a group's members than to have a leader who is guilty of vacillating. But they feel secure and know what to expect with a leader who is primarily consistent in his or her behavior. The leader who is democratic one time and autocratic the next, or who is tolerant of free discussion on one occasion and hostile towards it at the following meeting, will confuse the members and they will likely lose interest in continued participation.

As a leader, your best policy is to be completely honest with the members. If you make an error in judgment or find that you must reverse your position on an issue, you should make this clear to the members. This will contribute to their respect for you and they will feel more comfortable working with you.

Being consistent is extremely important when it applies to the leader of a group of children. While adults are more understanding and can appreciate human failings, children expect perfection. Where discipline is occasionally involved, you should be consistent in seeking the assistance of the group. They should expect to share the responsibility for the group and can participate in decisions when discipline is necessary. Whenever possible there should be choices possible in order that those who have done wrong can repair the damage.

The leader of a group of Camp Fire Girls found herself faced with a disciplinary problem when several members on a hike away from the camp came upon an isolated building in the woods and set fire to it. They said they didn't believe the building belonged to anyone and that it was an eyesore. Although the building was about collapsed, the owner was using it to store some field equipment. Fortunately, only a corner of the building was damaged and none of the equipment inside.

The guilty members were given the alternative of apologizing to the owner and paying for the damage or resigning from the group. They decided to face up to the problem. They went to the man's home and apologized for what they had done and paid for the damage out of their own pocketbooks, an amount of twelve dollars.

This was a serious situation, one that could have had a tragic ending. But how much better it was to give the girls the opportunity to redeem themselves with a lesson they are not likely to forget than to expel them from the group and hurt them perhaps permanently. The leader should remember that expulsion is the easy way out and does not contribute to the group facing its responsibilities. Of course, on rare occasions, there is no alternative to expulsion when the safety and rights of the group can be protected in no other way.

You should never use threats in order to maintain control of a group unless you are quite certain that you can and will carry them out. While threats should not be used indiscriminately, they are justified when they bring home to the group the rules and limitations which must be maintained. For example, in our case of the scout leader whose boys ran amuck throughout the farm, the leader would be right in making the threat that should this outbreak occur again the campout would be over.

A sensible and workable balance between the group's control and that of the leader should be developed. The leader should give the group as much responsibility for order and control as the members are capable of handling. Sometimes the group's control will be too stringent and will work a hardship on one or more of its members. When the majority of the members regularly attend meetings and keep up their dues, they can sometimes be intolerant of those who fail to do so. They may decide to kick a delinquent member out of the group. As the leader, on the other hand, you may suspect that the delinquent member has a reason for missing meetings and being behind in his dues, and you may believe that dismissal from the group would be detrimental or embarrassing to this person. Yet, you do not wish to condone delinquency, nor do you wish to take discipline away from the members. You might suggest that any action be postponed until the membership chairman, treasurer, or an appropriate officer could visit with the delinquent member.

Developing rules

It is the responsibility of the leader to assist the group in establishing only the rules and regulations necessary to carry on their business and activities. At times a group will establish such rigid regulations that the members feel little opportunity for free expression.

A volunteer service agency was in a constant state of conflict at each weekly meeting. The members were habitual breakers of the agency's rules. They would speak without recognition from the chairman, leave and reenter the room frequently, and carry on side conversations with each other during the meetings. Other members, meanwhile, would insist on living by the rules and were constantly trying to discipline the unruly members. These conflicts took up much of the time of the meetings and several members were threatening to quit if the meetings didn't start producing something besides arguments. Finally, the agency's president decided to take matters in hand. She met with the officers and together they decided to restructure the meetings, eliminating impractical and ludicrous rules, establishing free discussion periods, followed by a more formal period for taking action on issues. These ideas were presented to the membership. They unanimously agreed to the plan.

Some leaders have a tendency to be either too easygoing or too rigid. Either of these extremes distracts from the effectiveness of the group and tends to diminish active participation by the members. Usually, the exercise of common sense will dictate the amount of order, discipline, and control required.

The leader should approach the group with a positive attitude and a feeling of confidence. If you expect the members to be reasonable human beings who are thoughtful, considerate of one another and of yourself, they will usually not disappoint you. Your attitude toward them will in a large part set the stage for the performance—a meeting of cooperation and teamwork or one beset with conflict. If you are suspicious of the members, they are likely to return this attitude. But if you are enjoying yourself, this reveals a genuine sincerity in their interests and ideas, and chances are they will pledge you their support.

8 / Handling group discussion

From the standpoint of factual learning, the lecture method is as effective as discussion. There are sufficient experimental studies to demonstrate that the two methods are equally productive. A sharp distinction, however, should be made between the learning which results in remembering facts and the learning which results in changes of behavior. The discussion method appears to be more efficient in the latter type of learning. Over and beyond the factual knowledge and more important from the point of view of mental health, are the new skills in human relations that can result from participating in free discussion.

The value of free discussion

There is a rationale underlying learning by free discussion which you, as a leader of a group, will find helpful. An early change in attitudes can be evidenced by the reassurance that experiences and problems are shared in common by the group members. Expressions of this reassurance are frequently heard, such as the one that came out in a recent meeting when a father said, "When I heard some of the other fathers in the group tell of some of the problems they were having with their teen-age sons, I didn't feel quite so alone. If others had the same problems, I figured that maybe mine weren't quite as bad as I thought."

With this kind of reassurance as a foundation, thinking becomes more effective. The individual does not feel so hopelessly snared in his own unique problems.

One can sense in the statement of the father the release that he was beginning to experience. It is apparent that release is one of the important factors that does take place from time to time during free discussions. Ventilating one's problems can take the edge off anxiety and worry.

Another factor in the rationale of learning from group discussion is that for many people speech, in an atmosphere of understanding, is an aid to thought. This is illustrated in a meeting where a mother will make a statement such as was made in a discussion at a public junior high school. "The interesting thing was that as I discussed my problem with others at the meeting, a solution occurred to me. I've tried it and it seems to work." This is not an unusual case. Many of us have had similar experiences. We are having coffee with a friend and begin discussing some problem, and before we know it, we have found the solution.

Part of the rationale involved here is that the discussions have a definite problem-solving aspect. For example, a parent will describe his problem and other members of the group become involved and start suggesting possible solutions. At this moment, several members of the group are working on the same problem and the results are usually positive. This lends considerable flexibility to the potential solution to the problem. Not only has confidence been expressed that a solution exists, but the feeling grows that there may be a number of possible solutions.

The sharing of experiences contributes to the problem-solving aspect. Pooling knowledge and experiences can well produce positive results. The sum total of knowledge and experience of the entire group is in actuality so large that it would be difficult to measure. And when the pooled resources of many are placed at the disposal of a person seeking an answer, the results are usually positive.

Stimulus material

There is a variety of stimulating material which can be used as a background for group discussions. Films have certain advantages and are perhaps more appealing as they are directed toward both the eye and the ear. Films also provide an easy portrayal of dramatic situations.

There are also some problems posed by the use of films which we might mention briefly. While it is desirable for a film to stimulate the emotions and present an intellectual framework, there are some psychological films that may be too distrubing to many lay audiences. A film which creates even mild tensions should be followed by a sufficient discussion to give the members the opportunity to gain release from the tension.

There are a number of recordings that are useful as stimulus to group discussion. Large groups, however, sometimes have a difficult time in hearing the recordings. Recordings are more useful with small gatherings.

The summary of an article or a book or a newspaper item read to a group can be a good way to launch a discussion. Or perhaps you are good at telling anecdotes; this is a comfortable way of easing into a discussion. Depending on the group and the subject, sometimes merely a statement about the problem or the issue will get things rolling.

Apart from the question of what type of stimulus to use, nearly always in the mind of the leader is the question of what to do to get the discussion underway. Whether using a film, recording, article or anecdote, you will want to refer to some interesting point with which the material deals, but this introduction needn't be more than a few words.

A newly elected leader of a church fellowship group was conducting his first discussion. He had shown a film on the problems of drug addiction. The film ended and he found himself almost in a panic as he looked over the room of some forty boys and girls. Later he said, "If I had just thought about it ahead of time, I could have had several questions written on a card to get me started. As it was, without notes, I was stumped for something to say." He did manage to ask a question about the film. Someone came to his rescue with an answer and the discussion did get underway.

A few questions written down can be a real help, particularly to the inexperienced leader. The use of too many predetermined questions, however, may turn off the spontaneity of the members. One new leader wrote out a long list of questions related to a film, and the entire meeting was so structured that several members became so bored that they left early.

Another leader started out with a long list. She started asking her questions and received factual, disinterested answers in reply. Instead of continuing this approach, she was keen enough to push aside her questions, stating, "I had a number of questions jotted down but I don't think this is what we want to do. I am sure you have in mind some opinions or points of interest on these problems that you would like to share. I wonder if someone would start by sharing his thoughts?" The response was immediate and continued until the end of the meeting.

Once a leader gains confidence he will realize that getting a discussion started is usually not difficult and that any number of approaches will serve his turn. As a leader using a film, a recording, or an article as a stimulus, you might pick some debatable point in the material to get the discussion started. For example, the leader with the youth fellowship group might say, "The film made this a strong point against legalizing of marijuana. . . . What do you think?"

As the leader of a discussion, one of your objectives will be to develop freedom of expression and encourage spontaneity. Remember, however, that a certain time devoted to clarifying the procedure will be necessary in order to let the members know what is expected of them. They will be more comfortable and responsive if they know the rules of the game.

Clarifying the purpose

People coming together for a discussion—whether it is part of the activities of a permanent organization or a single meeting—will have a common goal, however vague. It will help if the leader at the beginning of the meeting outlines the purpose of the meeting. If the purpose or goal of the group changes, then the leader should clarify this modification, and it may be necessary to restate the goals from time to time. As goals are the framework for the meeting, they need to be thoroughly understood by the participants.

Although the general structure of the discussion meeting is understood, additional structuring is usually required. It might be advisable to say at the start, "We've come together this evening to discuss the need of a workshop for the mentally retarded children in our community. All of you have given this matter some thought. Our discussion will be most helpful to all if each one of you will give us the benefit of your thoughts and your experiences. And I am sure you have questions, and the group can assist you in finding the answers. Please ask questions. Relating your experiences to us and the way you look at some of these things will not only help us find the solutions we are looking for but may well supply a needed answer to someone here." The leader has let the participants know that they may express their feelings, relate their experiences, and ask questions. The structure for the meeting has been established.

You may find that you can put people at ease by saying something like, "Don't be afraid to express your thoughts. Sometimes those spur-of-the-moment thoughts are good ones. Sometimes they have little value, but let's not worry about that for we're here to brainstorm and do some thinking out loud."

It is highly desirable that a group establish its own standards to the extent that time allows. This is more difficult with a group conducting a short series of meetings than with one that has an indefinite existence. If the group can establish its own standards and structure, this helps establish a closer rapport between the members.

For a one-night stand or a short series of meetings, time can be saved if the leader will clarify the purposes for which the group is meeting and offer some suggestions as to how these purposes can be achieved. It is also in order if the leader suggests that certain procedures or objectives may be changed. The participants will feel that it is their meeting if the leader makes it clear that the meeting is flexible and subject to their wishes, as long as these suggestions are relevant to the general design and within the overall goals of the organization.

As a leader, you will discover that there are people who feel threatened when considerable freedom for individual expression is allowed. These people feel insecure at informal gatherings. During free discussion, you will occasionally hear people say, "We are not doing anything," or "We are spending a lot of time without coming to any decisions." You will learn to recognize the feelings which lie behind these statements and to accept them without feeling personally threatened. You may want to say something to them such as, "There are a lot of factors involved here and we want to be sure that we talk them all out. While we may not feel that we are getting anywhere right at the moment, these ideas will help us to solidify our thinking and arrive at conclusions later on." If the participant realizes that the leader is cognizant of this insecurity, he will likely be satisfied, at least for the time being.

The insecure participant who does not feel at home in a climate of free, permissive expression can often be helped by the use of a written summary. This provides something tangible and he feels that something definite has gone on and that certain things have been established.

Understanding roles

As a leader, you may wish to explain your role to the group. If you are a lay person, you may say, "As you know, I am not an expert and your opinions are as valid as mine, perhaps more so. In any case, I'm not here to express my own opinions but to help the group express its ideas. Certainly I'm not here to in any way pass judgment, but only to understand and sometimes clarify ideas if I can. I will be serving as a moderator and I will try to keep things balanced and to provide everyone a chance to say what he thinks. I will try to help pull things together in order that we can summarize and decide whether we have come to any conclusions."

If members of the group become confused as to what their roles are, it may be necessary to reclarify them from time to time. In time, the participants will learn to define their own roles and the roles of others. The constant interaction that will take place will help each member to know his relationship with other group members. This knowledge is sometimes referred to as process awareness.

Summaries

Depending upon the particular needs of the group and the type of discussion underway, there may or may not be a need to summarize. As a general rule, summaries are more often than not useful and welcome. But occasionally groups definitely decide not to summarize, feeling there are advantages in leaving questions open in order to stimulate further thinking. If the decision is for a summary, there are various ways to approach the task, and advantages and disadvantages for each.

There is usually a person in every group who enjoys—or can be persuaded—to keep a record of the proceedings and produce either an oral or written summary. When the group desires a summary but no one volunteers it, and the leader knows no one he can cheerfully draft, the only other choice is to rotate the responsibility among the members. This is usually not satisfactory. The members will be aware of this and what often happens is that some courageous member will say, "Well, look, I'm taking notes anyway, so I might as well try to put together a summary."

There may be times when you, as the leader, will decide that it would be well to ask the entire group to summarize. If it is not too large a group and there has been a balanced participation, this can be a satisfactory means of summarizing. The disadvantage is obvious —often the members do not restrict themselves to summarizing. They will start the discussion all over again on some interesting point. One way to handle this is to limit the amount of time each member has for his summary

It is not at all unusual for the leader to do the summing up. If you feel confident in this role, this at least eliminates the problem of recruiting someone else. There is also the added advantage of being able to direct the discussion toward the predetermined goal and gain closure, if needed. However, following your final summary it would be well to provide enough time to give members the opportunity to modify or add to your statements. Otherwise the members may feel that you personally are trying to control the meeting.

If a written summary is made, it would be well to provide a copy to each member. This will serve as his individual record of the meeting and it helps to understand the continuity. More than likely, the evolution of the group and the unfolding of its ideas can be found in the record. If a tape recorder is available, a record of the complete proceedings can be made. In my experience, however, the tape recording cannot replace the written record, but, of course, it can be extremely helpful to the person writing up the proceedings. Before using a tape recorder, you should make sure that its presence will in no way inhibit free expression. Tape recorders are so common these days that most people expect them at most meetings. Nevertheless, it is wise to check before using one.

Side conversations

As a leader, you will soon discover that the members will occasionally engage in side conversations. This isn't always because there's a lack of interest in what's going on. Frequently, members will break into side conversations with each other because of the great amount of interest developed around the topic at hand. Members may be so interested and their enthusiasm so great that they must express themselves immediately. It is natural that they turn to the person next to them, particularly if someone else has the floor at the time their ideas demand expression.

When a unified meeting breaks into numerous small ones, it is sometimes wise to let these conversations run their course for a time. Members will feel more satisfied if they can express their thoughts and feelings. It may be that they don't want to bring their thoughts before the entire group at the time. If the leader endeavors to squelch these conversations, immediately the members may feel he is trying to hold too tight a rein on the proceedings. They may resent this and it certainly can discourage free expression completely.

The leader must be the judge of how long to wait before calling the group back together. If side conversations continue too long, they may destroy the unity of the discussion. Frequently, after a few moments of spontaneous outburst, the members themselves will show a desire to return to the more unified discussion. As a general rule, four or five minutes is sufficient time for side conversations to last.

If the general meeting breaks into a number of side conversations and there are no indications that they will end naturally, you will be fulfilling your function as a leader by using any appropriate device to call the meeting back to order. If an intermission is due at about this time, it might be well to take the break earlier than scheduled. Intermissions should not last more than ten or twelve minutes. This is more than ample time for the members to visit and then return to business. If an intermission is not due, the members will probably not resent the leader calling the meeting back to order as they know that it's his responsibility to keep the group in pursuit of its objectives.

After the meeting has been called back to order, you can demonstrate your interest in what has transpired in the private talks by saying, "There were some interesting ideas going around while you were talking with one another. Would some of you like to report back on what was being said?" The group will feel good about what has happened and will see it as making a contribution to the proceedings. More than likely the content of these side conversations will indeed add something of value.

A more difficult kind of side conversation to handle will be that which transpires between two or more members who have a kinship with one another but do not have a sense of belonging to the group. Such conversations have a way of going on and on in an undertone while the rest of the group is endeavoring to carry on a unified discussion.

When this sort of behavior persists, it is disturbing to the group and particularly to others who sit near them. Faced with this problem, you would be justified in saying, "I feel that all of us would be interested in what you three have to say. Would you care to share it with the group?" You will need to make such statements in a friendly way. It should be stated as though you really believed they had something interesting to share with the others. Quite often, they will choose not to share their ideas—the conversation not being relevant to the discussion—but they will usually refrain from further conversation, having understood your message. Try not to be sarcastic or annoyed as this would only produce a negative effect.

If this attempt to bring those engaging in side conversations back into the group fails, chances are other members of the group will come to your assistance by showing their disapproval to these persons.

If you are a beginning leader, you may be appalled not only at the thought of getting the meeting started but at the possibility of a lull when everyone stops speaking and it is difficult to get the discussion going again. Once discussion groups are underway in a climate of freedom and friendliness, the enthusiasm is usually sufficient enough that lulls rarely occur. If they do, they are usually brief and the group will start of its own accord again with a new topic or a different approach to an old one.

Handling lulls

If a lull occurs and you become uptight or panicky, this will probably affect the rest of the meeting. Consequently, for your own peace of mind, it would be wise to prepare in advance for handling lulls.

Remember that a paue in the discussion does not necessarily reflect a lack of interest or an exhaustion of the subject. Members may be involved in some constructive thinking, a kind of creative pause. They may, then, resume the discussion with new ideas and enthusiasm.

You will become more comfortable as you learn to recognize momentary lulls. This ease will grow as you become more acquainted with the signs which indicate that members are thinking and not mentally asleep, and as you learn to use resources for getting the discussion going again if an actual lull does happen.

There are various things you can say to revive the discussion. After a pause has continued for some moments, you might venture, "Do you have some additional thoughts on this subject before we move along?'' If the members have been mentally toying with some ideas, they will advance them before a new topic discussion starts. If the members are through with a topic, you should be prepared to offer a new topic or some new aspects of the existing one. It sometimes helps to have a few ideas jotted down on a card. You may not need them but it is comforting to know they are in your pocket in any case. One effective and constructive way of getting the discussion underway again is for you, as leader, to give a brief summary of the discussion up to that point. If you don't feel qualified to do so, there may be someone in the group you can call upon.

The size of the group

It is difficult to establish a magic number for a perfect discussion group as so much depends on the organization, the issues or subject, the people attending, and the leader's ability. Of course, one doesn't always have a choice as the discussion may take place with an organization's membership which may be large or small, and attendance may be irregular. When a choice is available, a number between fifteen and twenty-five is usually thought of as being ideal. There are enough people for variety and not so many as to make the meeting unwieldly. If a meeting's activities center around discussion and a large number of people are expected to attend, it is usually wise to divide the large group into two or more groups. If one is not sure what the attendance will be, plans should be made for additional group leaders and adequate space.

There are definite advantages with small groups, even as small as four or five, as each participant is offered a maximum opportunity for expression. But this size of group may impose a limitation, a lack of variety in the discussion. The success of a small group will depend largely upon the resources of the participants. A handful of people who are enthusiastic about the discussion and have good rapport with each other may welcome the freedom of the small group.

Some small groups find themselves battling with the problem of morale. If this meeting is of any value, why aren't more people in attendance? The leader's satisfaction with the size of the group, large or small, will have considerable bearing on the outcome. Even though you are secretly disappointed, it might be wise for you to try to look on the bright side of the situation and make every effort to reflect this optimism as you work with the group.

While it has been said that twenty-five in attendance is a maximum number for an efficient discussion, there are certainly many exceptions to this. Do not be dismayed if you suddenly find yourself confronting forty people when you expected fifteen for a discussion meeting. Actually, the number is in your favor if you are a new leader. Consider the fact that these people represent a great variety of experiences and many sets of ideas. Get them moving with a few suggestions or preplanned questions and your worries will be over. The principal task in a setting such as this is to help the participants overcome any inhibitions they might experience by the largeness of the group. You may need to direct a question to some person in the group. While he may not be prepared to answer, chances are others will come to his rescue and, again, you are on your way. Once the discussion is moving along, your primary responsibility will be to referee and keep the few from monopolizing the discussion.

Larry M. was perplexed at the beginning of a series of PTA discussion meetings on mental health to discover that fifty-five people were planning to attend regularly. Despite the time consumed, Larry decided to give sufficient time for introductions and the learning of names. He discovered that after two meetings, a great deal of interaction was taking place between members outside of the actual group meetings as a result of the members' getting to know one another.

As the group was large, the discussion offered a great variety of points of view but had the limitation of providing less time for individual participation. Larry overcame this problem by dividing the participants into smaller groups from time to time. The more silent members discovered they could respond better in the smaller groups and this, in turn, gave them courage to speak out once in a while in the larger group. It might be noted that when it becomes necessary to divide a large group and additional leaders have not been recruited in advance, the best approach is to let the small groups choose their own leaders.

Sticking to the subject

The question oftentimes arises as to how much planning a leader should do prior to a meeting as regards the direction of the discussion. If the content of the discussion has already been determined, as is usually the case, how stringently should the leader seek to stick to this content? For example, if the subject for discussion is racial problems in the public school setting, should the leader keep the discussion within the limits of this predetermined subject?

While there is no specific answer to this question, it is safe to say that if the discussion is going to be spontaneous and allow for free expression, it will be very difficult for the leader to hold the group to a rigid or narrow line of thought. Considering the abovementioned subject of racial problems within public schools, if one begins with student attitudes, the group is bound to think of attitudes in terms of parental influence. This brings in the subject of the home, but who is to say arbitrarily that the issue of family attitudes is not part of the racial problem.

If, in such an instance, you, as leader, state, "We are not confining ourselves to our subject," you can easily imagine the reactions of the group members who will feel that they are being restricted in their pursuit of the subject.

If it has been decided in advance that a certain amount of time will be devoted to a subject and other subjects begin to come up, you need not actually inhibit the discussion but may respond to each subject as it arises, and from time to time summarize in order to illustrate the relationships. Although the discussion may have wandered far afield from the original subject, it more than likely will come back to it again and again. Doubtless, the summary will reveal how thoroughly the subject is being covered.

Allowing a great deal of freedom has many advantages and some disadvantages. To permit considerable free expression may mean that the group will sacrifice a degree of coherence and organization. Yet it's better to make some sacrifices rather than lose the interest of and discourage spontaneity in other group members.

Permissive discussion offers the advantage of giving the individual the opportunity to state his own experiences, to gain insights into his own behavior, and to discover the release that comes from defining anxieties and problems. An additional advantage is that an individual has the opportunity to gain new insights as to his personal, emotional, and intellectual development. He may gain further knowledge and development by expressing himself. It is impossible for an individual to jump emotionally from comparatively immature feelings to mature ones, nor from a place of limited information to a wide range of information. As a leader conducting a discussion, you must be tolerant of each participant and his level of emotional and mental development. The expression of emotions, recounting of experiences, and the verbal dramatization of these in a climate of freedom is important to learning. The individual has the opportunity to explore new possibilities and gain perspectives. With this kind of personal involvement, morale is usually high.

There is still another advantage to be gained from free expression in group discussions because participants usually arrive at their own solutions. During the discussion, they will be presented with a variety of solutions, none of which seems to be the exact solution, but the process of their thinking about these ideas usually brings them to their own solution.

As a leader of a discussion group, you should exercise considerable caution in suggesting to any member that he needs to be better informed. If the member himself requests information, then you can refer him to those resources you are acquainted with or to some person or agency that can be of help. Otherwise, it is wise to refer to resource material to the group at large.

The most effective way for you to learn about good group discussion is for you to go through the experience of participating in them. This will give you the opportunity of being a member of a group and gaining the knowledge of what kind of leadership is the most effective and satisfying.

Training in group discussion

A number of communities and organizations interested in developing competent group leaders have developed what appear to be successful programs. Potential leaders participate in actual group discussions followed by a period at the end for the analysis of those elements which contributed to a good or bad discussion. This critique serves to sharpen the perception of the individual in regard to the techniques and attitudes of the group leader. The potential leader learns what promotes maximum communication between participants, including the physical comfort of the group, the seating arrangements to insure communication, the leader's attitude toward group members, the way he responds and keeps individual participation balanced.

Organizations involved in training discussion leaders have discovered that it is effective to give potential leaders some experience in leadership soon after the study of the subject has begun. This increases the candidate's motivation and helps bring problems into focus. One way to initiate potential leaders is to divide the training group into smaller groups, each led by a trainee.

Another workable method of developing potential leaders is the use of role-playing, sometimes referred to as sociodrama. The impromptu plays require no prior planning. Several members simply voltunteer to play roles as members of the group involved in some problem such as getting a discussion started, failure of a group to concentrate on a subject, and so forth. The sociodrama is exciting and stimulating both to those involved and for those watching. In my experience, I have found this method is particularly good in developing young group leaders. The sociodrama is a tool which can be manufactured at the moment needed, for it takes very little time for the group to improvise a sociodrama and present it, unrehearsed, to the group.

Sociodrama has the added advantage of helping potential leaders better to understand their role and as they participate in the role-playing they learn how to use it with their own discussion groups. While there is nothing complicated about learning to use sociodrama, the name sometimes proves a barrier with some people. Sociodrama is actually something that lies within the experience of all of us. As children, we constantly used it in our informal play when we dramatized father and mother, cowboys and Indians, and so on.

Most people fall easily into the impromptu roles of sociodrama. It should not be confused with the more professional and clinical psychodrama. Sociodrama is simply an acting out of different situations that may occur within group discussions.

It is interesting to note that sociodrama is more dynamic than one might at first imagine. While it might seem that the participants would superficially act out their roles in a flat and uninteresting manner and find it difficult to manufacture dialogue, the opposite is usually the case. The participants generally become involved rather quickly. As they do not have to remember their lines, as in a theatrical performance, spontaneity takes over and the participants respond out of their life experiences or as they imagine how individuals would react to certain situations. Quite often, the participants become so involved that several may talk at the same time, true to real-life situations. Sociodrama is described in more detail in the next chapter.

These and other methods of developing leaders are well-known and are widely used by many professionals in the field of education. Assistance in the training of group leaders is available to organizations from several sources. A good place to locate a consultant is the extension division of a state university. If a consultant is not available at the time that assistance is needed, the extension service may be able to refer you to someone in or close to your community.

9 / Maximum group participation

There are some general techniques you should be able to use when necessary in order to insure maximum group participation regardless of the kind of meeting you are required to lead.

Good meetings are those which are interesting. Interest is such an important factor that we can safely say that your success as a leader will likely depend on your gift of getting and keeping people interested in what is going on.

Helping members to participate

Needless to say, thinking is the forerunner of effective action. Successful leadership consists of helping the members of your group define, state, think through, and solve their problems. As a leader, there will be times when you must act as the initiator, for you have the responsibility of getting the thinking process started and of guiding and directing it.

At the start of most meetings involving group participation, members will have a tendency to direct most of their remarks to the leader. Some will ask permission to talk, either by holding up a hand or by addressing the leader and waiting to be recognized. This is a natural beginning and will likely continue to some degree until the members have tested their freedom.

Depending upon the degree of structure, it is usually a positive sign when members start speaking in a normal conversational fashion. The discussion usually moves more rapidly and in a more stimulating way when this freedom is allowed. If the meeting can proceed according to the intended purposes and goals, there is no need for you as leader to intercept the conversations. You are justified, however, in coming into the discussion when some point needs to be clarified, when there is a need to draw the discussion back on course, to move along to additional concerns, to summarize, or to involve nonparticipating members.

As so often happens when the conversation is flowing freely, some members are doing most of the talking while the less aggressive members are having difficulty in finding an opening. If this is happening, it might be wise to break in at the first opportunity and seek the opinions of those who have not participated. Not infrequently a few members can become completely absorbed in the discussion of a subject foreign or boring to the other members, even though it may have some relevancy to the purpose of the meeting. It is then your job to ask the talkative members for clarification, and following that, you should guide the discussion back into concepts understood by most of the members. You might do this by saying, "Earlier there was a question which went unanswered," and in getting back to it the more aggressive members will not feel rejected.

If the discussion is to be of an open nature, you will try to avoid taking an authoritative role. Even if you consider yourself as an expert on the subject being discussed, you will turn your group off if you give them this impression. While they, too, may accept you as an expert, a prescription for the problem will tell them there is no need to continue the discussion. As most experienced people know, members may ask the leader for advice but they really don't want it. If someone in the group asks you a direct question, one of the best methods for dealing with it is to treat it as important enough for the group to consider. You can refer it back to the group quite easily. If members try to push you into a corner by saying something like, "But you haven't given us an answer," you may then wish to say, "Well, several points have been suggested by the group," and then you proceed to summarize. You may be able to counter with a question or suggest that the question remain open until additional opinions are offered. If you still feel you must give some kind of an answer, make it nonauthoritarian, such as, "Well, I have thought of it in this way . . . ." After as brief a statement as possible, you could conclude with a question, as, "What do you think?" If a member is merely seeking information, such as what committee a piece of legislation was referred to, and not your diagnosis, then it would not be inhibiting to the group to supply the information.

Buzz sessions

One effective method of gaining maximum participation in a large group is by way of the buzz session. You have experienced this when, attending a large dinner, you discovered that it was impossible to converse with everyone and settled for talking with those nearest you. This is a natural buzz session.

The sheer weight of numbers inhibits most of us from free expression. A group of six or seven people doesn't usually have this effect, but the pressure grows as the group becomes larger. The buzz session can take advantage of the fact that most people will converse in small groups.

One way to accomplish this is to assign each person to a small group prior to a discussion, which may be planned after a talk to the group by a speaker, the presentation of a film, or simply questions given to the group by the leader or chairman. Usually a certain amount of time is allotted for the buzz sessions. Each group picks his chairman or spokesman who will present the group's questions and statements. If your large group is assembled in an auditorium, you can have each series of three people in odd numbered rows turn and face those in the even numbered rows.

This approach is particularly effective when used in connection with forums and symposiums where several speakers deliver talks and questions are then invited from the floor. If the buzz session is used in a symposium, a certain amount of time—several minutes—should be allowed after each speaker in order that the group can formulate their questions for the question period.

In most cases, audience participation is increased considerably and the questions asked are much more intelligent. Further, there is less danger of encountering an embarrassing silence as sometimes occurs when the moderator asks, "Are there any questions?" In this case the moderator can turn to one of the groups and ask for a question or questions.

During many symposiums or forums when the buzz session is not used, participation is limited to those who enjoy attention whether they have anything to say or not or, perhaps, wish to show off their knowledge, and to those kind souls who feel compelled to ask questions to let the speaker know he is appreciated, and to the few who have contributions to make and are not inhibited by the large group. With the buzz session, every person in the audience has had the opportunity to participate and in a fashion which provides little discomfort.

With smaller groups, buzz sessions are not needed. However, in groups larger than eighteen persons where a problem of some magnitude has been presented and the larger group has tackled it for a while and is dead centered, then it may prove worthwhile for the leader to divide the group into smaller segments. He should restate the problem and ask the members to "buzz" on it for several minutes before coming back together. Oftentimes, the break and the chance to talk informally will unfold new ways of looking at the problem.

The buzz session has worked very well at workshop conferences. At the opening session, the chairman can divide the group into smaller units and give them problems and ask them to come up with questions and solutions which the larger group can attempt to answer.

Buzz sessions used in the closing sessions of the workshop conference have been used quite effectively. We are all familiar with a committee reporting to the general assembly. A spokesman for the committee reads his report and asks for its adoption. Someone seconds the motion and, with little additional consideration, the report is adopted by the assembly. This process is so drawn out and so dull that in order to get it over with the assembly is willing to adopt almost anything, and not infrequently does.

The buzz session, on the other hand, is a way of giving greater consideration to these reports. After the report is presented and the motion for its adoption is made and seconded, it is referred to the buzz groups for several minutes before the vote is taken. It is rather amazing how quickly inconsistencies, errors, and omissions are detected by the smaller groups that went unnoticed by the larger assembly.

Presenting problems

In order to place a problem before a group for its consideration, discussion, and action, the four most common methods are: 1) for the leader to present the problem; 2) to have some member present it; 3) to have the group select it by means of a check list; 4) to have the members act it out through role playing.

The most frequently used method, and perhaps the easiest, is to have the leader state the problem clearly, briefly, and as interestingly as possible. If you, as the leader, are presenting the problem to be discussed, you should offer it as a question rather than as a statement. If may be presented as an actual case which calls for action, or it may be a general outline of conditions calling for a broader conclusion. An actual case, however, is usually more interesting.

The leader might present a problem as follows: "We have been approached by a group of fathers of ten to twelve-year-old boys to sponsor them in Little League Baseball. You will recall that at our last meeting we discussed the possibility of sending some youngsters to summer camp. Would you wish to entertain both proposals or consider the merits of one against the other?"

Another issue might be presented as follows: "Because of the nature of our organization, the State Chapter on Mental Health is urging us to support Senate Bill No. 301. For those of you not familiar with this bill, it proposes (make a brief statement as to the essence of the bill or read the bill if brief). As you are probably aware, however, the State School Health Association is opposed to this bill and have approached us to take a stand against it. Would you favor a neutral position or do you think we should determine our position and take a stand?"

By way of gaining greater group participation, you may wish to involve the members in presenting the problems. Let us say, for example, that you are discussing the need for more employment opportunities for youth. Perhaps, then, early in the discussion someone says, "I would like to hire more teen-agers but my problems are . . . ." Here is the opportunity you need. Ask this person to come to the front of the room and to describe his problem. On a blackboard or on a large sheet of posterboard ask him to outline the important facts in one column and the possible courses of action in another.

After he has recorded what he can about his situation in each column, ask the other members for their solutions to this particular problem. Ask one of the members to record the suggestions on the blackboard. Request other members to present their particular problems and follow the same pattern. After you have received as many statements of particular problems related to the central question and as many possible courses of action as you can elicit, or have time for, you ask the members to consider whether or not they have clearly defined the problem of youth employment and whether they have determined any practical solutions.

Used by an alert leader, this approach of individual participation is effective in keeping the thinking of the group focused on the problem. While this is a guided discussion, the leader has never told the group what to think, only how. This method may prove to be too formalized and structured for some discussions. Nevertheless, it can serve as an excellent guide as to the direction that a discussion should take in order to involve the group members in the problem-solving process.

A problem checklist is merely a listing of a number of issues or concerns related to a broad problem. The list, while not exhaustive, is a way of defining and illustrating components of the problem. It provides the members a focal point from which to consider their own points of view about the issues.

Each member should be given a copy of the checklist at the start of the meeting. Ask them to check those topics which they would most like to discuss. When they have finished, read the list aloud and ask for a show of hands as to the subjects checked. Those topics having the most votes can be used first for the discussions.

This approach works very well in getting the meeting underway. All of the members have participated in the meeting from the start and, therefore, are more likely to continue to respond.

The use of role–playing for the purpose of presenting a problem to the group works particularly well when the members of the group are not adept at putting their thoughts and feelings into words. Teenagers, for example, usually gain more from role playing than verbal communication alone.

Role-playing simply calls for an unrehearsed acting-out of a problem by the members of the group. It has been used as a classroom device for children to present their understanding of a problem to either other children or to adults.

To be the most effective, the problem must involve people whose opinions and feelings can be defined by the group. There is no prior rehearsal and there is no script as the action and dialogue develops as the scene progresses. The drama should last only for a short time—a few minutes—or only as long as there is spontaneity on the part of the actors.

The first step in getting role-playing underway involves a warming-up process in which the problem is stated, the actors are selected by the leader and the members of the group to play the roles established, and the scene is set. The actors then give their unrehearsed version of the situation, each responding to the others. Following the presentation, the discussion anlayzes the action and the various roles and, finally, conclusions are drawn by the group on how to handle this and similar situations.

Sociodrama or role-playing can be used to present dramatically any situation involving two or more people. As group discussions center around human problems and needs, role-playing can be called upon to act out the situations or conditions under discussion. For example, let's say that the discussion concerns parental relationships with teen-age children and that the immediate consideration is how parents and offspring can sit down together to talk about use of the family car, hours to be home at night, smoking, etc. Perhaps at this point of the discussion there are a couple of participants who feel that parents should lay down the law and that children should have little to say as to decisions. There may be a couple of other participants who believe that teen-age children should be allowed opinions. The leader can then suggest that these discussants express themselves in a role-playing arrangement as they would if they were the parents or the children.

Chairs, table, etc., are then arranged at the front of the room—or, better, in the center of the group—and the actors take their places. The leader can suggest to one of the actors that he might get the drama underway by saying something to one of the others. For example, the father might say to one of the children, "You've been bugging me about the use of the car and I think we'd better reach an understanding right now!" Or one of the children might say to the father, "Dad, Joe and I would like to talk to you and mother about using the car more." The dialogue between the participants then continues until it runs its natural course or until the points have been dramatically presented.

An interesting arrangement and one that can be enlightening to both the participants and the audience is the switching of roles. In other words, have the actors switch from the parents' roles to those of the children and vice versa. Suddenly, the participants may find themselves arguing a different viewpoint and this can offer a new insight to them as well as to the audience.

Another example of the kind of discusssion that lends itself to role-playing is a conflict of interest situation. Let's say the discussion concerns a proposal on the part of a service-giving agency to establish a half-way house for recently discharged legal offenders in a residential part of town. This particular meeting has been called by the Bigtown Council on Crime and Delinquency to determine whether the members wish to support or oppose the proposal. The discussion has been lively. Some have argued that the establishment of a half-way house in a residential district would be unfair to the residents, offering a possible threat to them—real or imagined—and damaging to real estate values. Others have contended that the half-way house is badly needed and must be located in a residential area in order for the recipients not to feel that they are once again being institutionalized.

The leader at this point suggests that role-playing be used in order to illustrate better the opinions being presented. He suggests that the setting is a meeting of the board members of the service-giving agency planning to establish the half-way house, an ex-offender asked by the board to sit in as a resource person, and several residents of the area in which the half-way is being proposed. Roles are then chosen by the leader and/or the members and the role-playing gets underway with the actor playing the role of the chairman of the board asking another board member to comment on reasons for establishing the half-way house at the locations proposed.

Again, roles can be switched in order to widen perspectives and assist the participants in looking at both sides of the issue.

Role-playing can be used at scout meetings with the scouts playing the roles of the scout leader and executive committee members; at PTA meetings with parents and teachers playing each others' roles; at meetings on interracial relationships; at most any group discussion meeting involving human relationships. Role-playing can be particularly useful in training leaders, for it provides them the opportunity of understanding viewpoints and handling interpersonal relationships before they are faced with the real situation.

Role–playing has been demonstrated as a valuable tool in training people who are in direct contact with the public, such as teachers, salesmen, receptionists, social workers, clerks, etc. The approach has been used in many ways in solving various human relations problems. The technique lends itself so well to expressions, actions, attitudes, and feelings not easily described with words.

How people think

Leading a group discussion is for the most part a matter of helping the members to think through the problems and arrive at a conclusion. In order to do this, it is important that you, as their leader, have some idea how they think. Reviewing the thinking process will be of help:

(1) We recognize the problem. (2) We define, clarify, and determine the size of it. (3) We form an opinion or tentative conclusion as to how it might be solved. (4) We make every effort to get the facts. (5) We weigh these facts and modify our first conclusions if the facts so indicate. (6) We arrive at a firm conclusion based on the facts gathered. (7) We take the action indicated by the conclusion.

But we would be naive and certainly unprepared at times if we believed that all people at all times think along logical lines. Quite often people are guilty of scrambled thinking and some of their most common errors are the following:

(1) They fail to define the problem. (2) They start gathering facts without first forming a tentative conclusion. (3) They form an opinion or jump to a conclusion and ignore any additional facts. (4) They refuse to consider the facts in an objective fashion and revise their opinions as a result of bias. (5) They are unable to reach a conclusion even with all the facts at hand. (6) They reach conclusions but never act on them.

You will be hailed as a valuable leader if you will see to it that your group follows the recognized steps in clear thinking and assist them in avoiding the dangers of fractured thinking.

Preventing boredom

Interest, as mentioned earlier, is the key word to a successful meeting. The most piercing dart that can be thrown at a leader is that his meetings are boring. Prevent being known as a bore at any cost. Being interested is what keeps us alert and involved, and the question which you must repeatedly ask yourself is whether or not your members are really interested in what is going on.

As has often been said, interest is much like a fire. It is easier to get it started and keep it going than it is to rekindle it. And whether we like to believe this or not, it has been shown often enough to establish it as fact that while man thinks of himself as a creature of reason, he is largely controlled by his impulses. What this indicates is that we are not always interested in those things that our reason tells us we should be interested in. We are mainly governed by our emotions.

We can capitalize on these impulses, however, in several ways that will help to build and maintain interest in the group.

One thing you must do to get the members participating in what is going on as quickly as possible is to get them in the act. Before they have the opportunity to label the gathering as "somebody else's meeting," get them to thinking that it is their meeting, that they are important, and have roles to play.

You cannot elicit the interests of others unless you are clearly and visibly demonstrating your own interest. When one of the members is speaking, show your interest by giving him your undivided attention. Remember, your actions are going to speak louder than your words. Show your interest; don't talk about it. Interest and excitement are highly contagious. If the interest of several members can be won, it will quickly spread to others. And, of course, boredom works the same way. People in groups have a tendency to act the same way and, whether we appreciate this or not, we can make it work for us rather than against us.

By way of implanting and developing interest, it is well to identify during the early stages of the meeting those members who have already shown interest. You can get them involved by directing questions to them. They will likely respond with some interest and this will alert others. Don't take the chance of calling on the wallflowers at the start of the meeting. Wait until you have a lively discussion going before you reach out to the more quiet participants.

Don't forget the virtues of humor. Few meetings are of such serious intent that humor isn't a welcome guest. Humor helps us to relax, to be able to deal more objectively with serious matters, it helps people drop their defenses and become more responsive to others. This doesn't mean that you have to tell funny stories. Believe me when I say that unless you have a real knack for telling a funny story, avoid it like a disease. There is nothing that falls flatter than an unfunny funny story. No, humor is more of an attitude, a state of mind, a kind of visible cheerfulness. The natural laughter that comes from sharing the witticisms offered during any meeting will go a long way in bringing people closer together and foster a spirit of togetherness.

If you wish people to participate in the meeting, you'll have to make them feel important. All of us seek approval from others. The need to be appreciated is basic to human security and contentment. Take careful note of this and use it to your advantage. When a member makes a contribution, recognize him and give him credit. You will have gained a supporter.

A friend of mine coaches a Little League Baseball team and year after year he has an enthusiastic and winning club. Other coaches wonder how he comes up each season with such good players. His secret is the enthusiasm and dedication he engenders in his boys by showing his appreciation of them. He always manages to find something to compliment them on even when a workout hasn't gone too well. Because he believes in them, they believe in themselves, they have self-confidence and thoroughly enjoy playing ball.

The more you know about the members in your group, the more you will be able to make use of their experiences and knowledge. This awareness on your part tells others that they are important in your eyes. During the meeting, for example, you may be able to say, "John, you've had quite a little experience with the city recreation program. What do you think about these activities?" Use every opportunity to let others shine. You will be amazed how their interest expands. If you will reflect for a moment, you will recall that the gatherings which bored you the most were those in which you did not play an active role. A good rule to follow is to share the stage with as many people as you can.

One of those natural impulses to which we were referring has to do with curiosity. Most people are very curious about everything that is going on around them, such as turning around to see who has entered the room late. People's curiosity can be very distracting at times for a leader, but there are ways you can take advantage of this. I have known speakers who would bring all kinds of items to the podium, everything from musical instruments, which they didn't play, to boxes tied with ribbons, which they never opened. These were gimmicks but they did capture people's attention for they were curious about what was going to happen next. When speaking to a group, I like to have a blackboard with me when possible. I have discovered that drawing some kind of picture or diagram will provide the audience a focal point. Occasionally I will write a few words on the board and say, "Now that will help remind me to share a certain story with you later." Sometimes I don't get around to the story but mentioning it arouses their curiosity.

When you ask a question, it is wise never to mention a name first. Ask your question and then pause for a few moments before you name a respondent. While you are waiting to call out a name, glance about the room, picking out one face and then another. This pause alerts everyone and prompts them to think about the question. This builds suspense and for those brief moments they are all participants struggling to come up with an answer.

Another device for stimulating thought if a blackboard or poster-board is available is to put down several numbers instead of one at a time. For example, if you are calling for suggestions as to ways of raising funds for a club activity and a suggestion has been made, rather than just writing it down go ahead and write under it several more numbers. The additional blanks below the first suggestion will plant in the minds of the participants that there are several more suggestions which can be made. They will start asking themselves what they are.

Suspense can be a very strong interest factor. Suspense is what keeps us reading a mystery book to all hours of the morning. During a formal business meeting, conducted according to the rules of parliamentary procedure, it is the presiding officer's task to see that speakers for both or all sides of a motion under consideration are available. But in addition to providing a fair hearing this practice has another outcome. When the floor is given first to the proponents and then to the opponents of a proposal, the issue is kept in doubt. Suspense builds. Interest remains at a peak. This approach works as well during an informal discussion. If you can identify those persons who favor the various sides of a question, you can bring them into the action by rotation before any one side stacks up too much evidence. By maintaining an even balance in the arguments, you postpone closure, more information is presented, more people become involved, the suspense grows, and so does the interest.

Eliminating distractions

To gain a maximum amount of group participation, it is necessary to eliminate as many distracting influences as possible. It is difficult for people to pay attention to two things at the same time. If the chairs are uncomfortable, the room too hot or too cold, and there are disturbing noises outside the meeting room, the participants will be distracted from the matter at hand. As the leader it will serve you well if you plan to be at the meeting place ahead of time to check things out.

Yet, no matter how well you have planned a meeting in advance, some distractions usually occur. Telephones have a habit of ringing, members will show up late, the tape recorder suddenly won't work, the film breaks, and so on. While you cannot always eliminate the distractions, your ability to remain relaxed and to keep your attention focused will have a profound effect on your members. If you are prepared in advance for these distractions, you will be ready to handle whatever comes your way. In other words, assume beforehand that the projector may break down completely. You will be prepared to say, "Although we won't have the film, we have a great deal to talk about so we might as well move right into the discussion." In the case of late comers, you can use this opportunity for summarizing and restating the problem.

You put yourself in a position for a different kind of distraction when at the beginning of the meeting you pass out mimeographed or printed copies of reading material and then endeavor to carry on a discussion. This is a bad practice, for the participants will try to pay attention to you and to read at the same time. People just can't read, discuss, and listen simultaneously. If the reading material is important enough that it should be read prior to the discussion, give them time to read it. If it doesn't need to be read first, wait until after the discussion to pass it out.

One's attire can also be distracting. While it should not be drab, you can look sharp and be dressed properly for the meeting without overdressing. A leader should never endeavor to impress people with his or her clothing, as the audience will get hung up on what he is wearing and this is kind of a distraction. You can look well-groomed in your second best suit. While that noise in the adjoining room will probably cease after a few minutes, that flashy sports coat stays as long as you do.

A leader must learn to play many meetings by ear. He learns to sense the tempo, know when things are beginning to drag and that the pace must be increased. The correct balance of a successful meeting, conference, workshop, whatever, is largely a matter of timing. Good preplanning will help but so many things never seem to follow the script. Further, if the agenda is too cut and dried, too rigid, the participants will feel they are merely going through the motions and have little to say about the issues or activities at hand. There are always those who love to hear themselves talk and they are not always easy to cut off. Latecomers ask to be apprised as to what has happened earlier and what decisions, if any, have been made. For the sake of the other participants and your own scheduled activities, you have to keep things moving. In order to do this you may have to adjust your agenda, add something, take away something, diplomatically quiet some, while drawing out others. Experience, of course, gives us a greater sense of balance and timing. But a new leader can go a long way in establishing and maintaining control by keeping an eye on his own timing. He can keep his remarks brief and to the point and avoid repeating the contributions made by others. The leader sets the style of the meeting and the participants will usually follow his lead.

Nearly as bad as allowing the meeting to drag is keeping the same pace all of the time and the same routine. The same pace tends to minimize the suspense and the excitement of a meeting. Learn to sense this and to increase or ease up on the tempo. It is well to vary your procedure. If a discussion has been underway for some time and some of the members are showing restlessness, change the pace by summarizing, diagramming on the blackboard, dividing the group into smaller buzz sessions, introducing role playing, and so forth.

While the task of getting and keeping people interested is more of an art than an exact science, if you will familiarize yourself with the approaches and techniques described in this chapter, then you will be better prepared to exercise whatever flexibility is necessary to keep your members involved. Involvement is the secret to continued interest.

10 / Individual members

When working with people, one soon discovers the exciting and challenging fact that human personality is dynamic, not static, and that under the right set of conditions, changes in people will occur in constructive ways.

It is not an uncommon experience to see an individual who was a shy, timid adolescent develop into an active and charming adult, or watch an overaggressive person learn to be more sensitive to others, to learn to listen, and to work cooperatively with his fellow workers. Sadly enough, it is also not so uncommon to see a buoyant and promising person beaten down by life until all self-confidence is destroyed.

Reasons why people change

Changes in people do not happen without a reason. Some experience has changed their attitudes toward life and affected their relationships with people. The influence of some person or set of conditions has resulted in this metamorphosis.

One of the most important questions you will ask yourself, as a leader, is "Why?" Why is this boy withdrawing from the group? Why does that individual try to block everything that we do? Why does that person always have to dominate the situation? Whatever the behavior of the group members, the leader must recognize that the behavior is only a symptom of some underlying need. While you are the leader of the group and not their therapist, you can handle most situations successfully if you will try to identify the cause and then seek ways through the group and its individual members to meet this need.

We can learn our lessons in leadership in the many avenues of life. I once learned a valuable lesson while sitting in a physician's office in Denver. I had never been to this doctor before but went to him because he had been highly recommended by a friend.

Soon after I sat down and started glancing through a magazine I was shocked to hear the doctor's voice, booming through the walls into the waiting room, "When I tell you to follow my instructions, that's exactly what I mean. Now I want you to do what I tell you to do!"

The magazine fell into my lap and I started thinking that maybe I had made a bad choice. This man didn't sound very kind and sympathetic to me. Before I had the opportunity to contemplate the matter, however, I was shown into the doctor's office. I found myself facing a man who was pleasantly saying, "What can I do for you?"

I told him my problem—a painful throat infection—and for the next several minutes he examined me carefully while chatting in a friendly way about the kind of work that I did. He revealed a genuine interest in me, not only as a patient but also as an individual.

Yet no sooner had I started to put on my coat and leave the outer office than I heard him shout to another patient, "I told you to stop taking those pills, didn't I? Well, didn't I?"

I couldn't help but glance around the room at the other people. One elderly lady caught my glance and smiling, said, "Isn't he wonderful?"

I thought about this experience the rest of the day and I began to understand that this doctor was working on more than his patients' physical needs. Some of the people who came to him apparently needed to be scolded and treated in a domineering way. He didn't however, treat all his patients in that way.

The more one works with people the greater the realization that to work successfully with them one has to recognize their individual needs. What is appropriate behavior toward one individual may not suffice for another. As the doctor so clearly demonstrated, some people required that they be treated in an autocratic fashion, while others, such as myself, responded better to the democratic approach. Evidently we all went away happy, judging from the number of patients who were in his waiting room.

Relationships with other people

Much of your leadership with a group depends on your relationship with the members as individuals: how you respond to them not only as members of the group but also your interaction with them before and after the group meeting, during coffee breaks, etc. Behavorial scientists divide people into personality types. To interact successfully with the different types requires a recognition of the identifying factors. The following thumbnail sketches can serve only as the briefest of outlines.

The authoritarian

The authoritarian type tends to believe that his own language, country, town, and lifestyle is the best. He is usually rather narrow in his philosophy and tends to be very conservative in his economics and politics. Anyone who does not conform to the customs and manners with which he is in agreement is subject to suspicion. He dislikes what he sees as weakness and has little use for anything but strong leadership.

The libertarian

The libertarian type is usually somewhat an introvert who likes to be on his own. He usually displays self-confidence and prefers to be left alone to figure out the means once he knows the goal. More than likely he has a sharp, technical mind and is highly skilled at his job, and he enjoys challenges. He tends to resist what he interprets as control.

The egalitarian

The egalitarian type is usually liberal concerning politics, about the ways others think, and their lifestyles. He believes that persons must be judged according to their inner selves, the way they think and feel and react to other people rather than their race, religion, or creed. He doesn't like to be manipulated by others, nor does he like to see others manipulated. He resists the authoritarian approach but works well in a democratic setting.

The above three types are not, of course, distinct personality patterns in any complete sense, but they do illustrate most people's response to different kinds of leadership. If we recognize these traits in ourselves and others, it gives us a greater insight as to why some people happily accept our particular style of leadership and others resist.

There are other ways of studying and recognizing various types in our group. A wise leader will learn to identify different types and make use of the contributions they as individuals can make to the group. If, on the other hand, they are troublemakers looking for opportunities to take out their frustrations and hostilities on the group, our ability to pick them out gives us a better chance to handle successfully our interaction with them.

We can start to identify various types by focusing on the silent members and the overtalkative members.

The silent one

The silent individual has many ways in which he can contribute to the group. He may do an excellent job as a recorder, as a summarizer, or in taking care of the physical comforts of the participants, such as serving refreshments, arranging of furniture, and so forth. He may also contribute by operating a film projector or tape recorder.

You should not allow yourself to feel uncomfortable in the presence of a silent member for this will, in turn, be awkward for him.

Other members will accept this person's nonverbal participation as long as the leader does. If you can show that all persons are welcome and appreciated, this will put everyone at ease.

Most people would like to make comments before the group but either are too shy or believe they have nothing of value to say. You may be able to open the way for this person to offer a comment, but you should not do this unless you have some indication that he wishes to speak. If people do not wish to speak and you call on them, this places them in an embarrassing situation.

Some leaders have found it to be worthwhile purposely to engage these persons in conversation during intermissions or coffee breaks. Quite often they have comments to make that are quite useful to the leader. In any case, such efforts on the part of the leader let the silent member know that he is nonetheless appreciated. If the silent member has mentioned something to you of interest, you may wish to comment on this to the group, and this may be the trick which will draw him out. Even if this person makes no visible contribution to your group, who knows, he may gain something that he will share with others.

The overtalkative type

It is not always necessary to squelch overtalkative members—as people sometimes suggest—for they may be intelligent and experienced individuals who can make real contributions to the group, if you can control them.

I remember one leader's response to a person who was dominating the discussion. The leader said, "I think you have some excellent ideas and I'm wondering if it wouldn't be worthwhile for us to visit in order that we can pursue these ideas at greater length?" They met following the regular meeting and the talkative member conversed for three hours, as long as he wished without interruption. It is interesting to note that this opportunity to get some things off his chest made a difference in the amount of talking he did in the group. He continued to participate verbally but took only his fair share of the time.

You will find occasions when a member of the group has such

a pressing problem that he needs a lot of help. He may absorb a great deal of the time, but if the group accepts this need and responds to him, what one may witness is an effective use of the group focusing attention on a single problem. The group's ability to handle this situation indicates a mature group formation. The experience will probably be a positive one for all concerned. If this is what is happening, you would be wise to let it run its course.

On the other hand, if the members of the group are not in sympathy with the problems of the member and are showing restlessness, then you may have to interrupt and change the direction. We usually see this situation occur when the chairman of a committee has encountered some problems which his committee has been unable to handle adequately. He is asking help from the other members. Understanding his problems and seeing them as vital to the welfare of the group, the members may then automatically become a committee of the whole. However, if they, too, have problems or other matters to consider, they may resent the one member's domination of the time. As you can see, there are no hard and fast rules on this and it will be necessary for you to judge the situation as it occurs. If you remain in doubt as to what course to take, you may wish to refer the matter to the members for a decision. If there are issues with which they are not acquainted scheduled for this particular meeting, inform them of this and then let them decide.

One way to acquaint an overtalkative member with what he is doing to the group is to ask the recorder to read back the proceedings of the meeting. If the overtalkative member is at all sensitive, he will gain an insight and will inhibit himself for the rest of the meeting. In the absence of a record of the proceedings or any other visible means of turning off the overtalkative participant, you may have to suggest that some members have not had the opportunity to express themselves and then proceed to call on them for comments. You do not need to point directly to those who have been doing most of the talking. Also, you may wait for the talker to take a breath and jump in with, "You have raised an excellent point and I would like some other comments on this."

Each group has its cast of characters. You will discover individuals who invariably play the same role in one group after another, such as the person who time and again serves as secretary. They are good at keeping records, they enjoy it, and they are certainly the unsung heroes of every successful organization.

In contrast, you will find the villains, the "aginers," the blockers, the status seekers, and so forth. Perhaps without these helpers and the opposers a group would not be true to life. Let's take a look at some of these characters in our cast.

The orienting type

The orienting type keeps the group focused on the subject. He will say, "Let's remind ourselves what it is we are trying to accomplish," or, "Are we sure that is relevant to our subject? Perhaps we should review quickly what we have determined so far." He will keep track of the time and will insist on organization. While this is a role that you, as the leader, must be prepared to play, you are usually fortunate enough to have at least one other person in the group who is the orienting type.

The initiating type

The initiating type is always getting things started with new ideas and sometimes new problems. As soon as one matter is settled or an activity out of the way, he is right in there with his brain working overtime. As the idea man, he is invaluable to any group and a group of any size will have several such persons in its numbers. While he may present more new ideas than the group can act on, he is usually not discouraged if only one is selected.

The encouraging type

The encouraging type is the cheerleader of the group. He may not play an active role in the discussions or problem-solving, but he is an incentive to the group through his encouragement, show of approval, and appreciation of the work done by others. He may accomplish this with a smile, nod of the head, or other gestures. Occasionally you will notice someone make a statement and then glance toward the encourager for his approval.

The harmonizing type

The harmonizing type is usually embodied in that person who is mature enough to realize that the progress of the group depends on keeping matters on an even keel. He makes little effort to project his own ego or insist on the group adopting his ideas. Rather he encourages those who feel rejected, tempers those who become excited, and generally keeps the peace by serving as a mirror to others and reminding the members of the importance of the group function. When a discussion leans too far in one direction, he suggests that the other side should be heard, and he often relieves tension with humorous quips. A valued man in the group.

The clinging-vine type

The clinging-vine type is usually more noticeable with groups of children and youth than in adult groups. This person hangs on, sometimes physically, to the leader and is constantly at his side. Such an individual is obviously very much in need of attention. The behavior would indicate that the person had been brushed aside by others and it would be wrong for you to repeat this and increase the problem. Perhaps the best approach would be to show as much kindness and attention as you can without damaging the group. Possibly you can assign this person special duties which will indicate your appreciation of him. If the person is a child and is, for example, a member of your Girl Scout or Boy Scout troop, show as much attention as you can without indicating favoritism, subtly endeavor to get other members to involve this child, and keep the child busy with activities.

The facilitating type

The facilitating type keeps things moving and discussions from lagging by asking members to define their terms, to explain statements more fully, and calls attention to contradictions and failures to be objective. Being something of a "lawyer," he prevents premature closure on subjects and serves as a catalyst to the thoughts of others. Being a midwife to others' creativity, he can be of tremendous assistance to you. Without at least one good facilitator in the group, you must work much harder.

The recording type

The recording type is another valuable member of the team. Some people seem to be natural recorders in that it seems to be a psychological necessity for them to keep a written record of everything going on around them. You are fortunate if you have one of these naturals as the secretary or official recorder for the group. As such recording has probably been a habit of long standing, they have become experts at it and do an excellent job. If it is an informal gathering or a special committee without an elected secretary, quite often one of the participants will volunteer to take notes, commenting, "Well, I always take notes, anyway, so I don't mind doing it for the group."

The evaluating type

The evaluating type is constantly taking the pulse of the proceedings and an inventory of the progress. With his eye focused on the goal, he continues throughout the meeting to evaluate and weigh what has been accomplished, what remains to be done and what portion of the time is left to see the task through to fruition. When the discussion appears to be getting nowhere, he will come alive and likely say, "Well, we seem to have gone as far as we can with that line of thought. I wonder if we can try a little different approach?" And when things have moved along well, he will probably be the first one to suggest that a conclusion has been reached.

The analyzing type

The analyzing type is closely related to the evaluator and may well be the same person. This individual usually takes careful notes and may seek a structure or outline within which the group can work. He puts items down in columns, a kind of pro and con means of keeping track, and is a stickler for details, the absence of which he views as a hindrance to accomplishment. Some groups appoint one of the members to serve as analyzer-evaluator. He monitors and feeds back to the group the progress being made.

The summarizing type

The summarizing type draws together and integrates the ideas being presented by the members of the group. This ability, combined with the talents of the analyzer and evaluator, serves well to keep the discussion on target. When a group is interested in the discussion underway, there may be a tendency to wander astray of the subject, as a point of interest may well be a detour. The summarizer at such times serves as a centering device. No single member of the group makes a greater contribution than the summarizer. This is the task often required of the leader. It can be a difficult job if the leader is not familiar with the subject being discussed, so he can be extremely grateful for a good summarizer in the group. As a matter of fact, if you do not feel too comfortable with the subject to be discussed, it might be well to recruit a talented summarizer ahead or at the start of the meeting.

The humorist

The humorist may simply be a member who constantly sees the funny side of things. If he is a mature individual, he will not clown or slip into humorous remarks in order to draw attention to himself but will do so by way of making a contribution to the group. Such humor, if in good taste and correct timing, can be a valued asset to the group for it relieves tension, prevents members from taking themselves or others too seriously. The good humorist is an equalizer and harmonizer. He keeps matters in balance and offers a welcome change of pace.

The playboy

The playboy, on the other hand, is usually a distraction to the group. He is more interested in himself than the group. He displays a mild contempt for the leader and other members who make contributions by talking to others, interrupting the proceedings with horseplay or pranks. He may write out jokes and draw sketches which he shows to those near him. The playboy has never grown up and consciously or unconsciously he resents the knowledge and abilities of others. If the playboy is a child, he can sometimes be helped by being given a responsible task to perform.

The status-seeker

The status-seeker makes every effort to impress the group with what or whom he or she knows. He lets you know that he has all the answers and if, by chance, he doesn't have the answer, he immediately states that he knows somebody who does. He is a name-dropper and refers to conversations he had had with important people to whom he refers by their first names. His comments are delivered as though they were pronouncements and his manner indicates that he expects such deliveries to be accepted as though they were the last word.

The aggressive type

The aggressive type is a person who tries to get his way through bullying others. As a boy he threatened other children and used fear in order to get what he wanted. Although he is now contained in a man's body, he is no more mature than then. The only change in his approach is that rather than fists he browbeats others with ridicule and insults. Since he is an extremely insecure individual, you can usually keep him contained or under control by directing questions which can be embarrassing to him at those times when he tries to bully his way.

The monopolizing type

The monopolizing type is closely akin to others who demand attention from the group. He focuses attention on himself by a constant flow of words. He may start out to make a simple comment that ends up being a long dissertation on matters only slightly related to the subject at hand. You can depend on him speaking at every opportunity and to carry on ad infinitum and ad nauseam and even interrupting others to do so. He loves to hear himself talk and indulges his habit at the expense of others.

The expediting type

The expediting type shows concern for the comfort of others. He is aware of the setting of the meeting, the physical properties, the materials needed, the seating arrangement, and so on. He can serve a very useful role by being assigned the job of taking care of these matters, even the task of making the arrangements for the meeting, for equipment, refreshments, etc. The expeditor is a kind person, it is safe to say, and one who takes pleasure in doing things for others.

The fact-seeking type

The fact-seeking type never feels comfortable about arriving at conclusions until all the facts are in. When the discussions are rapidly moving along and some start making overtures that decisions need to be reached, the fact-seeker is likely to say, "I don't believe we can reach a final decision on this until we get more facts." There are times when such suggestions are bothersome but, for the most part, his plea is realistic as groups have a way of being carried along with their arguments which are not always based on fact. The fact-seeker may slow things down but he certainly contributes to sounder conclusions once they are reached.

The fact-giving type

The fact-giving type is that rare person who is virtually a walking encyclopedia. He can quote figures, statistics, and historical facts as though the books were in front of him. If he does not have the facts, he can quickly locate them for you. Generally, this person does not offer this information to call attention to himself or to gain status with the group; he does so as an honest contributor. He likes facts and has found that they can be extremely useful to a group. He remembers tax figures, budgets, etc., and can usually draw some comparisons which are useful. Certainly his role should not be underestimated.

The status-giving type

The status-giving type is a celebrity or individual of some importance in the community, state, or nation who is invited to become a member of an organization, association, center, because of the prestige he can give to the group. This is not an uncommon practice. Important persons who agree to do this usually only do so when they believe in the purposes and goals of the group. While it may not be openly so stated, there are rare occasions when these people fail to recognize the nature of the invitation. It is generally believed that there is nothing unethical or hypocritical about this arrangement as long as everyone is honest about it. However, there are those who criticize this practice on the basis that the celebrity will not play an active part in the organization and that he is merely window–dressing. Recently I questioned a national figure whose name has appeared in connection with several charitable organizations. I queried him about the use of his name and he answered, "Well, it is true that my schedule doesn't allow me to attend their meetings, so in that sense I contribute nothing. But on the other hand, I will not allow my name to be connected with anything I am not in sympathy with. I believe in the work of the organizations which you mentioned and if their directors feel that my name—my endorsement, so to speak— is beneficial to their cause then I welcome its use. That is my contribution."

The compromising type

The compromising type is the most agreeable member of the group. He is always willing to give ground, to compromise, in order to facilitate an agreement. This willingness to change his stand is indicative of a mature individual who is more interested in the progress of the group than in defending his own opinions. This virtue, of course, can be carried to a fault if he moves over at the slightest sign of disagreement, and other members will soon lose repect for his opinions, thinking, perhaps, that he is unwilling to stand up for what he believes.

The blocking type

The blocking type is the individual who is perennially against whatever others are for. This type of individual is difficult to understand but there always seems to be one in a group of any size.

Perhaps he imagines that his voice of dissent balances an overpositive stand by others. However, what usually happens to such a person is that his fellow members start "considering the source" and he soon finds himself ignored.

The whispering type

The whispering type is probably cut from the same cloth as the playboy and other attention-seekers. This person has hardly sat down before he starts a whispering campaign with his neighbors, much to the distraction of everyone near him. More than likely he will continue until someone says to him, "Excuse me, but I am trying to catch the drift of the discussion." Occasionally, a sharp look at him will turn him off for a little while.

The wool-gathering type

The wool-gathering type is an individual who seems to find it impossible to keep his mind on the subject at hand for more than a few minutes at a time. Long after the group has talked out a subject and moved on, he will be back at the middle of it somewhere. Perhaps the first item on the agenda had to do with the budget. This was settled and the group is discussing the appointment of a special research committee and the wool-gatherer asks quite innocently, "How does that compare with our budget last year?" As he apparently daydreams a lot, he may toss something into the discussion which has no relevancy with the subject or may ask time and again for something to be repeated.

The orienting, initiating, facilitating, encouraging, compromising, harmonizing, recording, evaluating, analyzing, summarizing, expediting, fact-seeking, fact-giving, status-giving types, and the humorist are various roles which contribute to the group process. Of course, some individuals play several roles among those described above.

The playboy, aggressive, clinging vine, monopolizing, status-seeking, blocking, whispering, and wool-gathering types are generally the undesirable roles played by people who tend to hinder the group process. Undoubtedly, there have been times when we have left our white hats at home and have arrived at the scene as one of the villains, and if not for the entire meeting, at least portions of it.

If at some time your group is discussing the group process, you might wish to try role-playing with the members depicting the above parts. A word of caution: Even if you believe that a certain person would be ideally suited to one of the detrimental or villainous roles because this is their usual role with the group, avoid making this selection. Feelings could be irreparably hurt and the purpose of the exercise would be defeated. If the role-playing exercise is carried out successfully, these people will be able to identify themselves.

11 / Informal groups

It is obviously important to use the type of meeting best adapted to the situation. The nature of the organization, its purposes and goals, the number of persons involved, the nature of the subject to be discussed, the nature of the project or activity, and even the type and size of the meetingplace will determine the kind of meeting best suited for the occasion. You would not use a butterfly net to catch an eagle, but many of us do unreasonable things in choosing procedures for meetings we conduct.

This chapter will be devoted to explaining methods of leading and presiding over various types of informal gatherings. These will include discussion groups, panels, symposiums, forums, interest groups, teams, the troop, or local unit of a national program organization.

Most people feel that the most enjoyable meetings are informal ones. Just as you probably enjoy yourself more at a backyard barbecue than at a formal dinner, so would you probably react better or be more like yourself at informal gatherings. Certainly, as far as developing ideas and being creative are concerned, the best work is accomplished in an informal setting where the participants are able to get to know one another.

The discussion group

The discussion group, or round table, is a gathering of usually no more than twenty persons; small enough that all can participate. All involved are considered equals as regards interest and knowledge of the subject to be discussed. You, as the leader, are another member of the group, the only difference being that you are responsible for making the meeting go, getting things underway, setting the stage, so to speak, keeping the group focused on the right questions, and summarizing from time to time in order that the members can know of their progress.

It is generally held that there are eight characteristics of the discussion group:

1. It is composed of persons who have mutual problems.
2. The members of the group believe there are benefits to be gained by solving their problems together.
3. The subjects to be discussed are well within the scope of their own experiences.
4. Members agree to share their ideas and pool their resources.
5. The problems are solved by solutions suggested and agreed upon by the group.
6. Members meet to work and learn together rather than to be instructed.
7. Individuals arrange themselves informally and usually face each other.
8. The group is small—usually from ten to twenty participants.

A small group of interested and concerned persons sharing common interests, believing that several heads are better than one, and arranged in such a way that no one is isolated is the perfect medium for democratic thinking and action. The arrangement is being used more and more for problem-solving for all kinds of organizations—civic, business, and professional groups.

It has often been said that life in modern society is group life, and that the individual who endeavors to go it entirely alone and gain results through his individual efforts may be handicapping himself unnecessarily. While we know that a skilled person may solve a technical problem in business or science while working alone, research has shown that group thinking may be more effective and quicker.

The everyday problems of schools, churches, organizations, municipalities are shared by all involved in a democracy and the people expect to think these matters out together. When the City Planning Commission is confronted with a zoning problem, the residents of that section of the city are called together to discuss the matter. The needs of a city park program are to some extent realized by all citizens, but the planning is referred to a group of representatives from interested organizations who recognize that they are representing all of the people.

Conventions, conferences, and other gatherings of large numbers of people almost always break down into smaller groups. This is where the real work, the actual thinking through of the issues, takes place. In large organizations of all kinds, the bulk of the work is done by committees, which are essentially small discussion groups. Large committees frequently break down into subcommittees, into units small enough so that all members are real participants.

As considerable space has already been devoted to the leader's role in leading discussion groups, I will add only the following outline of the tasks of the leader, recorder, observer, consultant, and group member as reminders:

The leader

- Helps the members become acquainted
- Establishes and maintains an informal climate
- States or has someone state the problem, or leads the group towards a statement
- Initiates, stimulates, and directs the discussion towards solutions
- Promotes the participation of all members

- Notes the contributions or progress of the group on paper or a blackboard
- Works for a balance of participation between members by encouraging the shy persons and tempering the monopolizers
- Stimulates the thinking process by asking if all sides of the question have been considered
- Helps the group take an inventory of directions and progress by use of the recorder and observer
- Offers a summary when necessary or, better still, encourages others to summarize
- Does not impose his own views and opinion on the group
- Helps the group to reach satisfactory conclusions and design a plan of action

The recorder
- Keeps a written record of the principal ideas, problems, and conclusions reached during the discussion
- Summarizes and provides a report at the completion of the session
- Reads back sections, statements, questions, and so forth, during the session as requested
- Prepares a final report of the proceedings

The observer
- Directs his attention to the manner in which the leader and the group members are operating and the progress that is being made
- Observes the degree and kind of participation by the members
- Observes the effectiveness of the leader
- Keeps his attention focused on the thinking and the attitude of the group
- Reports his observations to the group from time to time either when requested or when he believes they would be of assistance to the group, and usually at the close of the meeting

The consultant

- Provides facts and other pertinent information on the request of the leader or members
- Relates experiences when requested or when he feels it would be relevant and helpful to the discussion
- Helps the leader in seeing that all pertinent facts are introduced into the discussion and are considered
- Helps the leader in moving the discussion toward solutions

The group member

- Provides the group the benefit of his experience and knowledge
- Contributes ideas relative to the problem
- Plays various leadership roles as the need arises
- Pays close attention to what others have to say and appreciates their contributions
- To the best of his ability, avoids the extremes of saying nothing or monopolizing the discussion
- Refrains from allowing his own prejudices and ideologies from unduly influencing him
- Cooperates with other members in the group process and the solving of the common problem

The panel

The next arrangement for us to consider is the panel discussion, which is a means of informing a group on a particular subject by having a smaller group of experts informally discuss the subject. Usually, the panel is composed of persons who are better informed and have a wider experience with the subject than the audience. Not infrequently, however, the panel is chosen from members of the group or composed of the leaders or chairmen of small buzz sessions, held previously.

The panel discussion is the most effective when the audience can in some manner participate. When the discussion is either of a controversial nature or relates to problems shared by the audience, they should be allowed to direct questions to the panel members.

The panel consists of from five to ten persons and a discussion leader. If possible, the panel members should be seated in a semicircle in order that they may be seen by the audience and are able to see one another. The leader can be seated at one end or in the middle, preferably the latter, as he will then be able to direct the discussion better.

A panel discussion will be effective in many settings. However, there is a practical limitation to the size of the audience inasmuch as the discussion is carried on in an informal, conversational fashion. The audience must be close enough to hear clearly. Although microphones can be used, and often are, a problem still exists in that the panel members may not be able to hear questions from the rear of a large crowd. Then, too, the problem of hearing and making oneself heard tends to inhibit the freedom of communication.

Perhaps the best way to illustrate how panel discussions are arranged and conducted would be to describe one such program.

In this case, the audience was composed of about 150 police officers from small communities to large cities. The subject was, "How can we best make use of federal funds for comprehensive planning for delinquency prevention and control?" The general chairman—an administrative assistant of the governor—selected the panel members and invited them by letter to participate. The panel members consisted of the chairman of the state board of probation and parole, a district attorney, a state supreme court justice, an FBI agent, a judge of a juvenile court in a large city, a professor of criminology, and a police chief of a metropolitan area.

The chairman met with the panel members just prior to the meeting and outlined his plan for the discussion. He stated that he would ask two principal questions: (1) What practical measures could be used to improve the prevention and control of delinquency in the state? (2) In what ways could we best use the federal funds now available to carry out these measures?

He suggested that each of the panel members discuss the two questions in an informal fashion rather than as a speech. The district attorney was asked to take notes on the first question; the college professor was asked to take notes on the second question, and they were asked to serve as summarizers.

The meeting was held under the auspices of the governor's crime commission so the commission chairman introduced the panel chairman. The panel chairman acknowledged the introduction, stated the subject to be discussed, and led into the introduction of the panel members in the following way:

"I am going to ask each member of the panel to stand, give his name, and to tell you what his job is. I will start by stating my own qualifications. As the panel leader, I do not need to be an expert on the subject, and I truly qualify. The gentlemen seated here, however, are quite knowledgeable and I will now ask them to introduce themselves, starting on my far left."

After the panel members introduced themselves, the chairman stated the first question and allowed the panel to discuss it for about twenty minutes. He then requested comments from the audience regarding issues not presented by the panel. He asked for the summary of the question to be given by the district attorney. The second question was then introduced and after a thirty-minute discussion by the panel members, the audience was once again invited to participate. Following this, the college professor was asked to give his summary. The panel leader thanked the panel members and the audience for their participation and turned the meeting back to the program chairman.

This was an effective panel because the subject was of great interest to both the panel members and the audience. The panel members were informed individuals who could speak with experience and authority, and as the members of the audience were also knowledgeable persons they could and did participate in the discussion.

There are occasions when the leader of the panel is merely given a topic and it becomes necessary for him to draw statements of the problem as it relates to the audience from the audience itself. This can be accomplished in one way by using the buzz session mentioned earlier. The leader then states the topic, divides the audience into buzz groups, and asks them to determine what problems they would like to have the panel discuss. The buzz groups should be given a few minutes to decide and then to write their suggestions on a blackboard. The panel can then decide what problems to consider first and they can then start their discussion.

This approach can be reversed by having the panel members decide on what problems to discuss, write these on the blackboard, and have the audience decide in what order they are to be considered. Both of these arrangements provide for more audience participation than the panel discussion described. Yet, they take more time and it is quite possible that such a list of problems are offered that it is impossible to get to them all.

There are several things which you should try to avoid in using the panel discussion arrangement. Avoid being the focus of attention and feeling that you must always comment on the contributions of others. Make it clear that lengthy speeches are to be avoided and follow this practice yourself. Avoid stuffiness and rigidity by getting the panel on a first-name basis. Avoid any dress rehearsals with panel members as this will destroy the spontaneity. Make certain that you don't use all of your time for the presentation of problems and have no time for solutions. Be sure that you can point to some accomplishments, some closure, and the summaries will help on this. Avoid allowing anyone—panel or audience—to dominate the discussion.

The symposium

Panels are sometimes confused with symposiums but, actually, there is quite a little difference between these two arrangements. While panels involve several speakers on a single topic, symposiums have only a single speaker on each topic.

The effectiveness of the symposium depends largely on the degree of audience participation generated by the opening speech and how capable the leader is in stimulating an interaction between the speaker and his audience following his talk.

Generally, the symposium is more formal than the panel as the speaker will deliver a prepared speech. It is more easily used with a large audience. After each speaker makes his formal presentation, time is allowed for directing questions to the speaker. The next speaker then presents himself to the audience.

It would be well for you to ask the speakers to try to raise some questions about their subject rather than trying to supply all of the answers. As time seldom allows many members of the audience to present questions to the speaker, you might wish to divide your audience into buzz sessions. In this manner, all the people present become participants. Their spokesmen then present the questions to the speaker.

As regards the question-and-answer period with and without a buzz session, you can provide for this following each speaker or you can have all speakers make their presentations and have one longer question period at the end. There are advantages either way. With only one question period at the end, what so often happens is that most of the questions are directed toward the last speaker. If there is a period for discussion after each speaker, it will obviously take more time and questions may be discussed that tend to take away from what following speakers have to offer. One of the most effective arrangements, therefore, is to divide the audience into buzz groups following each speaker. Give them a few minutes to determine and write down their questions. They are kept until the question period following all of the formal talks and the questions are then directed to the various speakers.

The forum

The same principles can be applied with the forum. A forum has but one speaker and while he, therefore, can speak longer than with a symposium using several speakers, he should not attempt to answer all of the questions raised but should direct some to the members of the audience. This provides some areas in which the audience can probe and question.

A truly remarkable speaker who has the experience to gain rapport with his audience will more than likely find the buzz session unnecessary. He will have his own ways for drawing his audience out. But unless you are pretty sure this will occur, it is best to be safe and not gamble on the panicky emptiness that too often occurs when questions are requested but do not materialize following a speech.

The buzz session will guarantee that questions will be asked and they will probably be more intelligent ones than otherwise.

A substitute for the buzz session is the question box. The members of the audience are supplied with paper and pencils and asked to drop their questions into the box. The questions are read by the leader or program chairman and answered by the speaker. It is a workable approach but it lacks the spontaneity provided when the members of the audience ask their own questions.

One of the more informal structures is that of the interest group. This is a simple kind of group to lead and there is something tangible for the leader to work with, the interest in a certain subject or activity which has brought the members together. For example, a YMCA Boxing Club is an interest group, as is a college photography club, the League of Women Voters' state history group, and so forth. The interest in a particular activity may be the only bond welding the members together, although, of course, they may develop other relationships.

The leader of an interest group is usually chosen because of his knowledge in the field of interest to the members. Some leaders are highly trained and others have developed their skills through a hobby. The leader who is professionally trained, for example, in painting or music, will have a great deal to offer the participants but occasionally these people find it difficult to adjust to the informal setting where members attend mostly because they are seeking recreation. Some successful leaders know very little more about the subject than the members and might even plan to learn along with everyone else. Yet, if he or she knows enough to stimulate their interest and has good ideas on how they can pursue their common interests together, this enthusiasm will more than make up for his lack of skills.

The special-interest leader must be concerned with the development of his members as well as the teaching of a subject or skill. This is particularly true when the group consists of children or adolescents. The leader must serve in the dual role of being a teacher and a leader. There is no conflict between roles if properly understood.

In his role as a teacher, the leader is involved with helping members learn how to carve, take pictures, build birdhouses, act, and so forth. He is teaching them skills but he needs to be interested in what is happening to the member as an individual. Rather than just imparting information, the leader should be interested in developing the individual's creativity, and helping him use his own ideas. Some leaders make the mistake, in their zeal to have their members make better objects, of losing sight of how much creating something can mean to a person.

The teacher-leader who ignores or breaks a ceramic dish a child has made because it wasn't turned out according to the instructions and exclaims, "You just aren't listening," may well be destroying the youngster's creativity and self-confidence. Anyone who ever created anything has put something of himself into the object. The good teacher will not condone mediocrity but he will help the individual to improve his or her skill. It is usually better to praise the effort and then show how it might be done better, indicating at the same time a belief that the person can do better.

I was acquainted with a coach of a junior high football team who had discovered that he could get boys to live up to their potentiality—maybe more—by the use of sugar rather than salt. When a player made a half-hearted tackle, instead of shouting at him he would say, "Now I think you're getting the hang of putting that shoulder down so next time go ahead and hit as hard as you want to." His philosophy seemed to pay off for he always had a crowd come out for football, they won ballgames, and also learned some important lessons in living.

In his group leadership role with young people, the specialist teaching some skill or activity is also helping the person to work in a group and to learn to live with others.

The group process

As leader, there are a number of things which you can do to initiate the creative group process. Be sure that the members become acquainted and that there continues to be communication among them. This can be accomplished by having them work together on a project and by staying long enough at the end of the session to help clean up.

A mistake frequently made by persons serving as leaders of interest groups is that they imagine that others have the same degree of interest as themselves. As this may be their only field of interest, they expect others to display the same dedication. While this may be true of some members, many more will have other interests, and if this person is going to work with interest groups, he has to be concerned with their development as people and not just as devotees of his special interest.

The team

The team is a type of interest group and as used here refers to those other than which are part of a public or private school activity. Team, within this context, usually means a group formed to take part in various athletic contests such as Little League Baseball, church basketball leagues, etc. Organizations sponsor the teams selected on the basis of age, size and sometimes skill in order to provide fair competition.

The leader in this setting is referred to as the coach. He teaches the players how to play the game, how to work together as a team, and if he is doing a job of helping the players develop as people, he will be more concerned with teaching fair play and sportsmanship than in winning games. In view of the greater needs of the players and the higher purposes to be served in leading a team, the coach will see to it that all members are given a chance to play regardless of their skill.

The coach will find it necessary to watch closely for intergroup conflicts which can result from the stress placed on competition. Some coaches have discovered that conflicts are more infrequent when the players of the two teams have become acquainted. Social gatherings after games when the players get together for cokes and cookies have proved successful. Particular attention needs to be directed toward cooperative interplay when the teams are from different racial or religious backgrounds.

The club

The role of the club leader differs in a few ways from that of the leader of the special interest group. However, as a leader of either group you are concerned with helping the members have a creative growing experience. With the special interest group, it is the common interest that has brought the participants together.

The club members, on the other hand, simply wish to be together and enjoy themselves. As the leader of a special interest group, you know what it is that interests them and your job is to use this interest in helping them to function as a group. As the leader of a club, your task is to discover the kind of activities which will interest them the most.

In the beginning, you will probably have to plan a varied program until you discover their interests, and, if they have had little experience in the group process, you will have to bring them gradually into the planning. You start with the members, get to know them, where they are, what they are like, and what they want to do.

The formed group

A somewhat difficult small group to lead is the formed group. This group structure occurs when the members have been brought together by some organization or agency and the group is determined by age and sex. Examples of the formed group are church Sunday school classes, YMCA and YWCA children's activities groups, summer camps, city recreation programs, day-care centers, and neighborhood recreation programs. Some of the members may know each other but they usually have not been together as a group. Most of the members will not know each other.

As the leader, you must get to know the youngsters, help them to become acquainted with one another, discover their interests, and teach them to work and play together as a group. With this type of group, we might say that you are starting from scratch. Obviously, then, you must play a dynamic role.

In the beginning, you may need to start your program and base your planning on some assumptions as to what a group of this size, sex, age, backgrounds are usually interested in. You can then modify from time to time with their assistance. One of your first tasks is to ask the members to come up with a name for the group. This will immediately get the members to thinking in terms of the group.

The troop or local unit of a national program organization, such as 4-H, Camp Fire Girls, Boy Scouts, Girl Scouts, and other such groups, are actually a combination of the special interest and the formed group. Usually the members come together because they wish to be a member. These are interest groups because the organizations have a well-defined program that the boys and girls must follow in order to be members. While the activities they will be involved in will be varied, the principal interest is in doing those things which are at the core of this type of group. The national organizations have established certain requirements that must be fulfilled by the chapters, the leaders, and the members. However, they are to be seen as the framework within which the group has quite a little freedom. As the leader of such a group, you will wish to take advantage of the training courses offered by your organization and to use the excellent program guides developed by the national office.

12 / Formal meetings

The formal business meeting plays an important role in our social structure and way of life. It is generally carried out according to parliamentary procedures. As so many organizations follow this design, you are more likely to be asked to lead a meeting of this kind than of any other kind previously described. It differs from informal gatherings as it is conducted along the lines of parliamentary procedure. Nevertheless, most rules and approaches for effective leadership are applicable regardless of the structure of the group.

In presiding over the more or less formal gatherings, you will discover that years of tradition have established a clearly defined order of business. It is necessary to fully understand these orders of procedure. You will also find that you have more authority both expressed and implied than one does when leading most informal groups. Most of your members will be familiar with parliamentary procedures and will expect you to follow them. Deliberations follow recognized rules of procedure, and result in formal recorded action. Formal proposals are made, discussed, voted upon and recorded.

To fulfill your position as the leader your first responsibility is to become completely familiar with the rules of procedure in general use and any modifications traditionally used by the organization. These will be your tools, your guidelines around which you will structure your leadership efforts. The bible for parliamentary procedure is *Robert's Rules of Order.* A copy can be obtained at your library or, if you prefer your own copy, it can be purchased at most bookstores.

Once you have learned the rules of the game, you will be able to go through the motions. This chapter is devoted to describing the leadership qualities you can learn to bring into play within this framework.

Principal responsibilities

Your principal responsibilities for presiding at a formal meeting include initiating proposals for the group to consider and bringing before them issues on which they may wish to take action; facilitating the deliberations of the members in order that they can conduct the business for which they have come together; guiding members in carrying out the business of the organization; encouraging and supporting a climate of harmony and teamwork; clarifying and summarizing motions offered for consideration before they are voted on by the members. The formal business meeting, as with discussion groups previously mentioned, utilizes the democratic process during the discussion.

To initiate matters means to bring up those issues which need to be considered by the group. This responsibility you share with the other members, but, of course, as leader they will expect you to do more than your share of keeping track of the issues. It is always well to do some preliminary planning before a meeting and if there are sufficient issues, it might be well to hold a prior meeting with the other officers as an executive committee. This can help you anticipate items which may be offered from the floor. Going over the minutes of the last meeting with your secretary will help you take inventory, and this should be done in sufficient time before the regular meeting to obtain whatever information or resources you might need.

While you are considering the order of business, you will more than likely discover several items which you can initiate as the presiding officer. The order of business generally accepted is as follows:

1. Call to order
2. Reading of the minutes of the previous meeting
3. Treasurer's report
4. Introduction of guests
5. Reports of standing committees
6. Reports of special committees
7. Old business
8. New business
9. Program
10. Adjournment

You set the stage for the initiation of business in carrying out the above duties. Let's say that you've called for the report of the membership committee and after the report is made, you state, "Thank you. You've heard the report of the membership committee. Are there any questions?" You pause and then add "If not, what is your pleasure concerning it?"

You have provided the members the opportunity to participate by means of your questions. Be prepared to initiate action by asking, "Are there any questions?" "Is there any discussion?" "Is there any unfinished business?"

To facilitate is probably your most important responsibility. No one gets too excited over formal business meetings. They can be pretty dull even for very active members, and most participants like to get through them as quickly as possible. They'll love you as their leader if you can take care of the business efficiently but rapidly. This can be done if you keep things moving along and following are a few hints.

Hints for exciting leadership

Know your parliamentary procedure so well, along with other traditional items peculiar to your organization, that it becomes automatic.

Even though you have learned the procedures well and may even be an old-timer at the game, it is wise to have a parliamentarian. Appoint someone to this role for one very good reason if no other: regardless of how well you know your stuff, sooner or later some member will challenge your procedures and if you have someone else to glance at the book besides yourself then this takes the monkey off your back, i.e., you aren't put in the position where you antagonize the member by being a greater authority.

Keep things moving. After a decent pause, when you have asked them if there are questions, move on to the next order of business. Don't belabor a question. The members will soon realize that if they wish to respond they will have to speak up quickly, and they will appreciate this approach. We often hear people say that life has a beat or rhythm. If so, this certainly applies to business meetings where a sense of timing keeps the members alert.

By all means, avoid long explanations, for your task isn't to give facts and explain everything. That's the responsibility, for the most part, of the committee. Your responsibility is to initiate and facilitate. Anyway, most members will feel you are insulting their intelligence by way of lengthy explanations. Note that if you have to be the fact-giver, be the last resort. There may be an occasion when during a discussion on a motion you feel so strongly on some point that you must enter in. All right, this being the case, turn the chair over to the vice–president and enter the discussion as any other member would, but don't do it as the presiding officer.

To keep things moving along, use your secretary. He or she should be briefed on items of unfinished business from the minutes of the last meeting. Work with your secretary in order that he or she can be adequately enough prepared to get the motions down on paper as they are made, and be ready to read them quickly to the group when requested to do so.

Keep your eyes on the members as much as possible. If you are not familiar with the procedures and do not have the items of business clearly in mind, you will find yourself constantly studying notes and papers. This will prevent you from watching the action around you.

As the presiding officer of the organization, you have real authority, so use it. Do not abuse it, but use it. Remember, in a formal business meeting, no one can address the group unless they have gained the consent of the chair. You are the one who determines when a matter will be brought to a vote, and you decide whether a motion has passed or not. That gavel handed you should not be an idle tool.

By way of keeping things moving, use the procedure of handling business by general consent whenever it is appropriate. This procedure can be used whenever a matter under discussion obviously has the unanimous approval of the members. Rather than going through the procedure of asking for a motion, a second, discussion, and a vote, you can bring the matter to a close by simply stating, "It appears to be the consensus of the group that we do this and this. So, if there are no objections, it is so ordered." Gaining the approval of the minutes of the last meeting can usually be done in this manner. For example, in this case, you could state, "You have heard the minutes of the previous meeting. Are there corrections or additions?" You pause and then add, "If not, they stand approved as read." The reports of standing committees often can be handled in this fashion.

Most business meetings move along in an orderly style; motions are made and passed and there is little excitement. That is until the day that you find yourself in the middle of different kinds of motions and requests for changes in motions. For example, most motions require only a majority vote, but some require two-thirds majority. Which are which? To confuse the issue more, there is rank among motions. "Privileged motions" are at the top, "subsidiary motions" are next, with "incidental motions," "renewal motions" and "main motions" following in that order. When do they occur? In what way can the wording of a motion be changed without amending it, or withdrawing it? Further, let us suppose that someone makes a motion, someone else amends it, and another member moves to amend the amendment? It happens. How long can this go on and how do you stop it? How do you go about taking action on all those amendments? Things can get out of control easily.

It is at such moments that you can appreciate a good secretary and an experienced parliamentarian. A successful job of guiding and orienting the group often calls for good teamwork. Find a good parliamentarian, be sure he or she has a copy of *Robert's Rules of Order,* and is seated beside the secretary so that together they can pull you out of tight squeezes.

One of the most common errors a leader makes is to allow a discussion to take place prior to a motion. This may seem reasonable but it is incorrect parliamentary procedure. When a discussion starts, you should ask that someone put the discussion into the form of a motion. It is then seconded and the discussion can get underway. After an adequate discussion, during which you have endeavored to keep the sides balanced, you can ask for a vote. The person making the motion should be allowed to discuss the issue first and, incidentally, the person making the motion doesn't necessarily have to be in favor of its passage but merely wants it to be discussed. You should try to alternate between those in favor and those against the motion and no person should be allowed to speak twice before others have had the opportunity to speak once.

A difficult problem of importance to the group should be given sufficient time for discussion so that the members feel assured that all facets of it have been presented. In order to do this in a way that all members, including the timid ones, have had adequate opportunity to express their views, you may find the buzz-session approach worthwhile. If there is not sufficient time for the matter to be talked out to the members' satisfaction, rather than push for premature closure it might be well for you to suggest that it remain open until the next meeting when it can be reintroduced under old business.

In order to keep things moving in interest of effective action, you should be ready to summarize a discussion and bring the matter to a decision. As mentioned, sometimes action can be taken by general consent, in which case you would summarize quickly and state that it would appear to be agreed that certain action is indicated and that it is so ordered. When you call for a vote, restate the question or have the secretary read it aloud, and say, "Are you ready for the question?" and then put it to a vote.

Working with committees

As you probably know from having served on several committees, a great deal of the business of a formal group is done through committees. How well the various committees function determines, largely, the success of the organization. In establishing and working with the committees, try the following rules:

1. To the best of your knowledge, appoint those persons who have a real interest in the work of that particular committee. Don't always look to the same active persons and don't overlook new members, for their interest in the organization will likely depend on how involved they are.

2. When making your appointments, ask yourself if these individuals will be able to work together successfully as a team.

3. Discuss the work of the committee with the chairman in order that both of you are clear as to expectations. If possible, committee assignments should be put in writing.

4. Once the chairman and his committee understand the assignment, allow them to take the responsibility, for nothing is more defeating than to be assigned a task and then be constantly reminded how to do the job.

5. You can ask the chairman for progress reports from time to time, but hands off other than that.

Items to be remembered

Following is an outline of some things you should keep firmly in mind:

1. The reports of committees can be received, or accepted, or

approved. The report that is received has been heard but not necessarily approved. The treasurer's report should be recieved, not accepted or approved. A report of the membership committee outlining projects to enroll new members may be accepted if the group approves the proposal. You should not ask for reports to be accepted or approved unless you intend to bring them up for adoption.

2. A nomination does not require a second.

3. Motions must be made and seconded *prior to* and not after discussions.

4. Restate the motion after it has been made and seconded and initiate the discussion by asking, "Is there any discussion?"

5. Only one main motion should be considered at a time.

6. A main motion brings an item of business before the members for action. It is the lowest ranking but the most common motion.

7. A privileged motion is one that involves immediate action by the group, for example, that they recess or adjourn, and is the top-ranking motion and therefore not debatable.

8. A subsidiary motion is one to change, postpone, or dispose of a main motion. It ranks below a privileged and above a main motion.

9. An incidental motion has to do with the method of conducting business, such as a point of order, method of voting, etc. It must be disposed of before the motion which precipitated it.

10. A motion can be changed without being formally amended by motion by requesting the maker of the motion to change the motion to include the suggested change. If he agrees and no other member objects, the motion is changed.

11. If a motion to amend is made and seconded, it must be voted upon prior to voting on the motion to which the amendment pertains.

12. A motion to reconsider must be made by a member who voted on the winning side when the original motion was carried.

13. It is general practice for the person presenting a committee report to move that the report be accepted. If he doesn't do this, you should ask him if he wishes to do so.

Common usage

Following are several statements of common usage in presiding over a formal meeting:

1. When you call the meeting to order: "The meeting will please come to order."

2. When asking for the minutes of the previous meeting to be read and approved: "Will the secretary please read the minutes of the last meeting?" "Thank you. Are there any additions or corrections? (Pause) If not, they stand approved as read."

3. When calling for reports of standing committees: "We shall now hear the reports of the standing committees. Does the program committee have a report to present? You have heard the report of the program committee. Are there any questions? (Pause) If not, the report will be received as read."

4. When calling for reports of special committees: "Are there any special committees which are prepared to report?" Are there any questions concerning this report? (Pause) If not, what is your pleasure concerning it?"

5. When considering old business: "We shall now consider old business. Madame Secretary, do we have any motions pending from the last meeting?"

6. When considering new business: "As there is no additional old business, the chair will now consider any new business."

7. Handling a main motion: "You have heard the motion. Is there a second? It has been moved and seconded that we purchase a new microphone. Is there any discussion?" After the discussion, "Are you ready for the question? The question has been called. All those in favor of the motion as stated (repeat the motion if necessary) signify by saying 'Aye.' Those opposed signify by saying 'No.' The motion is carried."

8. When a member rises to raise a point of order: "State your point of order. Your point is well taken. The motion is out of order."

9. When adjourning the meeting: "This completes the business of our meeting and the chair will entertain a motion to adjourn.

It is moved and seconded that we adjourn. All those in favor say 'Aye'; those opposed say 'No.' The motion is carried and the meeting stands adjourned."

10. Remember always to speak of yourself as the "chair" and of the other officers by position rather than by name.

We have discussed most of the tools you will need as presiding officer and the rest—the skill and tact of presiding—is a matter of practice.

The thousands of service clubs—Lions, Kiwanis, Rotary, Optimists, and so on—located in the towns and cities here and in many other countries provide a tremendous social and community service. They not only provide millions of men and women social and professional contacts but also a means whereby interested citizens can work together for the welfare of society.

Most of the service clubs elect a new president each year and if you are an active and devoted member you will likely sooner or later be called upon to serve your club as the chief officer. If this is your year, some of the following suggestions should assist you in being a success.

Guidelines used by service clubs

Guidelines used by several service clubs offer the following suggestions to presiding officers:

1. Establish a plan and timetable for each meeting.
2. Always operate as a team with your secretary, tail-twister or sergeant-at-arms, song leader, program chairman, etc.
3. Promote and maintain fellowship by giving the members a good pattern to follow.
4. Keep things moving and from time to time provide a change of pace.
5. Foster member participation.
6. Be familiar with the objectives, functions, and policies of your club and conduct your meetings accordingly.
7. Above all, be yourself.

Let us take a closer look at each of these objectives. As regards planning and the use of a timetable most service club meetings have three phases:

1. The fellowship period when the members have the opportunity to visit during breakfast, lunch or dinner.
2. The president's time, the period reserved for the affairs of the organization, special reports, announcements, etc.
3. The address or feature of the day's program.

In drawing up your plan, you should include the timetable and the details for carrying out each of the three phases of the meeting. An outline might include these steps:

1. Call to order

    (a) National Anthem
    (b) Pledge to the Flag
    (c) Invocation

2. Meal service
3. Introduction of visiting club members and guests
4. Announcements
5. Club singing
6. Special features
7. Introduction of the chairman of the day
8. Introduction of the speaker
9. Acknowledgement to speaker
10. Adjournment

It wouldn't be such a bad idea to take an outline such as this, modified to meet the needs of your club, and have mimeographed copies made to last you for the rest of the year. Then prior to each meeting you can take the outline, pencil in the changes, add the name of the speaker or feature, and you are prepared for the meeting.

Operating with your team made up of secretary, tail-twister, music chairman, program chairman, etc., can well be the secret of your success. Use them well and regularly. For one thing, many service club secretaries serve for years and if yours has, he or she will have more experience than anyone else in the club. Make use of this talent and knowledge.

It might be well to get to the meetings early. You can eat early and be ready to handle the affairs of the meeting. If you can get the other members of your team to come early, you can familiarize them with the agenda.

You should work with your music chairman in using imagination in song selection and the singing activities. Generally, an enthusiastic singing club is an active club so don't overlook the use of this particular activity as a means of fostering fellowship and morale.

Promote fellowship by establishing the climate yourself. The fellowship period should stress friendliness to all and efforts should be made to recognize and speak to all members. Establish the habit for your club of making guests feel welcome. The friendliness should not be forced or overdone, but it should be natural and open. There is little room for stuffiness or false dignity in a service club. And the very worst thing you can do is give the impression of self-importance.

The clubs that are successful year after year are those with a tone of joviality without being riotous, where there is fun but not boisterousness, and where serious matters can survive without heaviness or stuffiness—an atmosphere in which people can relax, enjoy each other's company, and discuss matters of common interest and of benefit to the community.

With good planning and a timetable, you can keep things moving at a healthy clip. Don't slight a portion of the program or skip over matters which should be attended to, but keep activities from lagging by thinking ahead. Keep alert and your attention on the group, for they will tell you whether you are moving too slowly, or too rapidly. If they act confused and seem unable to follow what is happening, chances are you need to slow down. If they are yawning, looking around, whispering to their neighbors, you need to speed up or change the pace.

While the members are going to be aware of the basic schedule, never allow activities to become so routine that they will be able to predict what is going to be said and to happen next. This is fatal as they won't have to pay attention, or even attend, for that matter. Change the pattern and pace and get this message over to your song leader and/or your program chairman. For example, it isn't essential to have a speaker for every meeting. Break off the routine by "booking" a musical group, a magician, a scientific demonstration, etc.

It will add interest and a change of pace if you will vary your procedure in introducing visiting members and guests. Introductions needn't be handled the same way each time. You can have the visitors and guests introduce themselves or you can have the member sitting next to a guest introduce him. Variations can be found if you are willing to look for them.

When you visit other clubs, keep an eye on the various things that are done, the novel procedures that are used. While it may be routine with them, It may not be for your club and can offer an interesting change of pace. Ask other members to keep alert for new ideas when they are visiting.

One of the secrets of every successful service club is member participation. People tend to be more Interested when they are involved, when they are participants and not just observers.

Promoting member participation

Here are some suggestions for promoting member participation:

1. Make maximum use of your officers and board of directors. See to it that they are assigned every responsibility consistent with their positions. During board meetings, you should see to it that everyone becomes involved in the discussions and that it doesn't become simply a matter of you reporting to them.

2. Every member of the club should be on at least one committee.

3. Be sure that your program chairman, music chairman, and sergeant-at-arms understand their jobs and are carrying them out.

Don't make the all too frequent mistake of doing their job for them.

4. If you can get your program chairman to assign as many members as possible to the job of planning the program for at least one meeting during the year, this will foster broader participation.

5. An interesting change of pace that involves the members is having two or more meetings a year with program devoted to group discussions. You could make up a panel selected from the membership. Also, you might consider using your members as occasional speakers.

6. Members can be assigned to introduce speakers and guests and you might wish to provide them with some written instructions. The following is an example:

(a) Relax—the members are with you.

(b) Feel happy and express yourself as though you are.

(c) Make what you have to say brief and enthusiastic.

(d) You should talk a little faster than usual.

(e) You should talk louder than usual unless using a microphone.

(f) If you can be funny, that's great, but don't try it otherwise.

(g) Speak as though you were talking to a friend and avoid reading if at all possible.

(h) Relate personal things about the speaker which were not covered in the advance publicity.

(i) Give the speaker's name at the end of your introduction. Speak his name with force.

(j) Initiate the applause as the speaker rises and you should remain standing until he acknowledges his introduction.

In order to function smoothly and effectively as the leader of the club, it is important that you are completely familiar with the policies, functions, and purposes of your club. Even if you are an old-timer with the group, it is nevertheless wise to get all of the literature available from the club's international headquarters. A careful reading of this material will give you a fresh perspective on the organization's goals, history, trends, and so forth.

Finally, your success as this year's president will rest on your ability to remain yourself. It was you that the members elected president and it is you whom they wished to do the job. As you look back, you will recall other presidents, some who did their job exceedingly well and others who left something to be desired. To the best of your memory you might give some thought as to why some were more successful than others. These points might serve your turn. Chances are that as you turn these factors over in your mind, you will discover that the successful leaders always acted themselves, before and after they were president. You will also find that their talents, though successfully used, were not the talents of another successful president. Dick Smith didn't try to be Harry Jones. Add up your own talents and skills, don't be envious or try to imitate someone else's, and use what you have. When you are just yourself, you are relaxed, natural, and less likely to get in your own way.

13 / Conferences and workshops

Conferences and workshops have become an important adjunct of business and professional life in modern society. Most active persons in either business or one of the professions attend several conferences and workshops each year—locally, regionally, nationally or internationally. Most attend for a variety of reasons. Many of them go because it is expected of them. It would be safe to venture, I think, that most expect to have fun at company or agency expense and this is viewed as one of the fringe benefits, and it is a way to take a short vacation on company time. A large percentage welcome the opportunity to renew acquaintances and value highly the business and professional contacts they have made. There are even some who hope to gain information from the official meetings.

You frequently hear people say that they gain more from the bull sessions and informal gatherings in hotel rooms than they do from the conference sessions. In such cases, at least the conference can be given credit for making such unofficial gatherings possible. But I feel reasonably certain that many conference and workshop attendants have become caught up in conforming to a stereotype of using the conference as a chance to live it up while away from home and at company expense. Judging from recent conferences I have attended and my interviews of persons immediately following official sessions, I would say that not only are the largest percentage of registrants attending the sessions, but they are also collecting useful information.

Conferences and workshops do not have to be painful and boring experiences. They can be grueling if participation is limited to a few principal speakers, presenters of papers, panel members, and a handful of respondents. Such gatherings force those in attendance to sit long hours listening to others declare how they discovered answers and solved problems. While all of this may be worthwhile information, it wears thin after a few hours and it isn't any wonder that many wander off somewhere to more personal involvements with friends. They are active people and many are not geared in a fashion that allows them to be only observers for long.

Directing our attention first to conferences, if you find yourself responsible or partly responsible for the planning of such a gathering, the following suggestions for conducting good conferences might prove useful:

Effective conferences

1. Make it a work conference in order that those in attendance are not only talked to, but have the greater opportunity to talk, to think, to discuss, and to arrive at conclusions and decisions.

2. See that the principal purpose is planned group action designed to offer new ideas, share information, and bring about some concrete changes in the field and in the attitudes of those involved.

3. See that the focus remains on problem-solving rather than on the presentation of concepts, particularly abstract themes. This factor should be made clear to speakers, panel members, and other participants.

4. Remember that the conference should be concerned with the problems and needs of the delegates and not those of the leaders. They are not always synonymous.

5. Bear in mind that the conference should have a clearly defined action objective and that the conference agenda is designed to move steadily toward that objective.

6. Allow time for relaxation and enjoyment. The delegates will be much more willing to attend and to actively participate if sufficient time is allowed for rest and play. If leisure time is not provided, the delegates will take it anyway. Such a development fosters nonparticipation and eventual loss of interest in the proceedings.

7. Provide for the mechanisms and the means whereby not only the leaders but the delegates are able constantly to evaluate the progress being made.

8. See that little time is spent on speeches of welcome, introductions of persons known to everyone or of no great interest to most, formal papers, and speeches of any kind unless the speaker has something important to say on relevant problems and is someone the delegates are anxious to listen to at some length.

9. Be certain that you utilize the leadership qualities of the delegates, and utilize as teams the discussion leaders, recorders, observers, summarizers, and consultants.

10. You should plan for a variety of group activities and meetings. When you can, divide larger groups into smaller groups so that participants can become involved in working with the conference theme and in problem-solving.

11. Carefully plan the final day so as to avoid an anticlimax. Organize well, in order that the final sessions are the highlights of the conference, the culmination of all that has gone before, and has been leading up to this point. The final sessions should provide the summaries and the conclusions, including those which have to do with implementation of recommendations. Delegates should be sent on their way fully informed as to what steps to take when they get home.

A successful program

A study of a successful program should provide us with some guidelines for planning and running a good conference. The following program was a three-day affair and it was attended by approxi-

mately 200 delegates. After looking over this program, we will analyze it somewhat. The delegates felt it was highly successful and
voted to plan next year's conference around the same format.

State Peace Officers Association
Juvenile Problems Conference
November 1, 2, 3, 1974

Wednesday, November 1
8:30—Registration—Auditorium, Universal College
9:00—Opening general session, Auditorium
   Chairman: Henry C. Hall, executive director, State Peace Officers Association. Recorders: Cecil B. Turner and Betty Hawley
   1. Greetings to delegates, Robert Frank, president, State Peace
      Officers Association
   2. Conference announcements and business
   3. Address: "Problem-solving In 1972-1973," Hon. Raymond
      S. Roberts, justice, State Supreme Court
   4. Buzz groups to select problems for discussion by panel

10:30—Intermission
10:45—Discussion by panel of problems raised by Justice Roberts
   and suggested by buzz groups.
   Panel Members:

   Hon. Raymond S. Roberts, justice, State Supreme Court
   Robert Frank, president, State Peace Officers Association
   Herbert T. Crowley, assistant attorney general
   Richard B. Conner, director, State Department of Social
      Welfare
   George E. Schultz, director, State Highway Patrol
   William T. Karman, district attorney, Metro County
   Discussion Leader: Henry C. Hall

12:00—Luncheon, Universal College Cafeteria
 1:45—Second General Session, Auditorium

Chairman: Mark B. Twilly, administrative assistant, governor's office. Recorders: Helen F. Jones and Pearl C. Barnes
1. Address: "Can Control of Juvenile Delinquency Become a Reality?" Frank F. Chambers, chief, Children's Psychiatric Program, Werner Foundation
2. Buzz groups to select problems for discussion by panel

2:45—Intermission
3:00—Discussion by panel of problems raised by buzz groups
Panel Members:

John O. Plank	Howard E. Evans
Franklin E. Parks	Eugene D. Stoker
Steve D. Dores	Alice P. Ownsby

Discussion Leader: Frank F. Chambers

4:30—Coffee and Fellowship Hour

Thursday, November 2
9:00—Third General Session, Auditorium
Chairman: Dr. Willard T. Awner, director, Sociology Department, Universal College. Recorders: George H. Hogan and Floyd R. Sealy
Theme: "Tools To Do The Job"
Keynoter: Hon. Leland F. Floyd, majority leader, State Senate
Panel Members:

Leo L. Bruner	Lynda R. Richards
Stanley C. Acorn	Allen D. Smith

10:15—Intermission
10:30—Section Meetings
12:00—Luncheon, Universal College Cafeteria
1:30—Section Meetings. Continuation of morning sections
3:30—Intermission
3:45—Fourth General Session, Auditorium
Chairman and Discussion Leader: Hon. Thomas A. Alan, judge,

District Court, 5th Division. Recorders: JoAnne D. Derby and Robert F. Menns
Panel Members: The panel will include one recorder from each of the six discussion sections

4:40—Adjournment
6:30—Association Banquet, Student Union Banquet Hall

Friday, November 3

9:00—Fifth General Session, Auditorium
Chairman and Discussion Leader: Donald F. Greer, director, State Board of Probation and Parole. Recorders: Nancy M. Yates and Dwayne J. Dirks
Theme: "Interagency Planning"
Panel Members:

Ralph J. Mocks	Dorothy H. Hand
Jane T. Bates	Donald G. Fleck
Kirwood R. Kitch	Marvin H. Eastman

10:15—Intermission
10:30—Section Meetings
12:00—Luncheon, Universal College Cafeteria
1:30—Section Meetings. Continuation of morning sections
3:00—Intermission
3:15—Sixth General Session, Auditorium
Chairman: Dr. Bernard D. Walker, associate professor, Department of Criminology, Southern State University
Recorders: Shirley K. Owens and Lee H. Davis
1. Reports from Friday sections
2. Address: "Methods of Implementation," Dr. David D. Grawling, superintendent, State Division of Public Instruction
3. Conference evaluation

4:30—Adjournment

By way of analysis, then, let's take a look at the following:

1. Formal addresses were limited to four—actually, three, for one was a summary of the conference. All speakers were excellent.

2. All of the formal speeches were followed either by a panel, buzz session, or both. The delegates had the immediate opportunity to discuss what was said within the framework of the conference itself; not just in the hotel rooms.

3. All delegates were provided the opportunity to participate throughout the conference. They could voice their opinions and discuss the major problems of the conference. Many were involved as recorders, panel discussants, and section leaders.

4. All meetings, activities, speeches and discussions centered around the problem of juvenile delinquency and what could be done about it.

5. During at least one-third of the conference time, the delegates were divided into six small work groups. Each of the groups spent three and one-half hours discussing some facet of the major problem of the conference. The conclusions reached were reported in general meeting.

6. No speeches were given at the banquet. Instead, an excellent toastmaster served as master of ceremonies and offered a program of entertainment. The food was good, the group enjoyed themselves and appreciated the use of the banquet for fellowship—pleasure and relaxation rather than as a medium for imparting additional information.

7. Business and play periods were scheduled. All meetings started at nine o'clock in the morning and were adjourned at four-thirty in the afternoon. Mid-morning and mid-afternoon intermissions provided for coffee breaks. The only evening session was the banquet and it was over with early in the evening.

8. At the close of the meeting, the delegates were invited to judge the conference and to offer suggestions for the next conference.

Examining the planning that went into the conference, we discover that three committees consisting of several experienced persons assisted the general chairman. The theme was determined a year in advance, as next year's conference was determined at this year's conference. One of the three committees handled physical arrangements, registration, rooms, and so forth. A second committee planned the meals and entertainment. And the third committee planned the program. Several months in advance of the conference, delegates were requested by letter to suggest certain aspects of the major theme which they would like discussed. Their suggestions were summarized and became the problems discussed by the smaller groups. A preliminary meeting was held with the discussion leaders, recorders, and panel leaders to brief them on their responsibilities and functions. As they were well–informed, they were prepared to function as a team at the conference.

This conference plan will fit into one, two, three or more days of meetings. Conferences are still being held which are planned and dominated by a single leader. In my experience, however, they are seldom, if ever, successful. A better and easier road to travel in planning a conference can be gained by following these suggestions:

Planning pointers

1. Plan a *work* conference by involving as many persons as possible who are interested in its purposes and goals. Delegate responsibilities to these people, for there is absolutely no reason why one person should be burdened with the hundreds of things involved in planning a conference. Implant the notion of "our" conference and recruit a number of assistants, each with his own duties and tasks, but working together as a team.

Establish committees for each of the major components of the conference—physical arrangements, including facilities, rooms, meals, registration; a second committee for special events such as banquets, entertainment, tours; and a third to be in charge of planning the program, recruiting speakers, recorders, panel members, and other personnel. With large conferences, you may wish to divide the work among more committees.

By way of involving more people during the conference, use panels and symposiums rather than speeches whenever possible. Divide the group into small enough sections until the groups are small enough for round table discussions. Provisions should be made for the small groups to report back to the conference.

2. Start planning next year's conference at the completion of this year's conference. As a matter of fact, if you are to be next year's general chairman, you might plan to hold a preliminary planning session with several of the individuals you wish to involve immediately following adjournment of this year's conference. Although the last-minute rush can't be entirely avoided, it can be alleviated somewhat by getting your teams working early.

3. Involve the members in planning your program and establishing themes. This can be done by asking your program committee to write to the members and ask them to list the problems they are interested in discussing.

4. The conference theme should be constructed around problems rather than topics. Topics tend to be too vague or abstract. People are involved in problems and not topics. The conference should consider the real problems people are involved in and endeavor to work out the solutions. When your program committee contacts the members regarding their interests, they should ask for problems and not topics. Problems can be discussed and answered for they stimulate the formulation of plans for doing something about them. Topics, on the other hand, are usually viewed as subjects to be discussed but not acted upon.

5. Plan for adequate time for all scheduled events, actually a little more than you would appear to need, for conferences have a way of falling behind schedule. There are delays: people fail to show on time, it takes additional time to make introductions, somebody talks longer than you had planned. If you fall behind schedule, activities become hurried and confusion sets in. Provide time for intermission or coffee breaks.

6. Better to have fewer speakers but good ones. Do not patronize people by placing them on the program because they hold a certain prestigious position. In order to satisfy a few, you may disenchant many. Rather than mediocre speakers use some other approach—panels, symposiums, etc. Even a good film is better than a poor speaker. What so often happens at conferences is that for

welcoming addresses, keynote speeches, the governor suddenly can't make it and so he sends along his third assistant and no one is interested in him. There is nothing, of course, at that point that you can do but let the man speak. If you really want the governor, or the mayor, or the senator, fine, as most of the members would probably enjoy hearing them speak, but unless you can be assured of the man himself, it is best to cut down on the speeches and get on with the job at hand.

7. Whenever possible use your own members as panel or discussion leaders, section leaders, recorders, consultants, observers, and in other jobs. This kind of involvement really makes people feel that it is their conference and not just one they happened to attend.

8. Keep the conference moving along briskly until the final adjournment. If the final day or final session is an anticlimax or the work has been completed, or maybe petered out, the delegates will likely consider the whole conference as somewhat a waste. If you use your time well, then you will need the final sessions for reaching conclusions, solving problems and making some recommendations as to how the solutions can be implemented.

Conclusions can be reached by having an offical observer head a panel made up of section observers or leaders, who bring into the final sessions the written reports of their sections. The reports are discussed by the official observer and the panel members and then the discussion is thrown open to everyone present. The reports and points of discussion can be summarized and included in the conference report.

Knowing what needs to be done at the conference is a major accomplishment by itself. Then there are the practical things that can be done by the individuals, agencies, institutions, to implement any changes deemed necessary. I have seen some really excellent conclusions reached at conferences only to discover later that little was accomplished on the home front because the delegates didn't come up with any concrete plans for implementing the changes the next time. The final session, then, should be reserved for this purpose. It might be well to seat a panel of persons selected for their experience in the field of implementation, or if necessary, bring in outside experts. The panel should be well-acquainted with what it takes to get action from city, county, state or national governments, to change agency policies and regulations, to gain cooperation between agencies, to bring about in-service training and educate the public, and whatever else.

A really successful wind–up of a conference is when the delegates head for home inspired to make changes and have the knowledge of how to accomplish them.

The workshop

Let us now turn our attention to workshops which are similar to conferences in many ways. The workshop has come into popular use by many professional groups as a means of providing short-term intensive training. Several days—sometimes longer—are devoted to bringing together experienced persons with common problems for the purpose of working out solutions. They are assisted by leaders who are sometimes drawn from the group itself.

The workshop is a work session, as the name implies, and it is carried out in a democratic fashion with all members equally involved in problem-solving. It is larger than a discussion group but basically the same otherwise. Most workshops involve too many people for a single group and so they are usually divided into sections. Each section, then, concerns itself with a facet of the larger problem. The workshop is similar to the conference but it is usually concerned with fewer problems and gives greater attention to those problems under consideration. Speakers usually are not used at workshops.

Let us consider a successful workshop by way of illustrating arrangements and methods proved to be effective.

This workshop was conducted by the state vocational education department and held in the facilities of the state office building. It was held for five days and was attended by fifty persons from a seven-state area. All the participants were involved in program planning for their respective states. Their problems were common ones and their backgrounds similar. The state director of vocational education in the state where the workshop was held served as general chairman and made all the physical arrangements. The directors of the seven participating states recommended persons to act as chairmen, recorders, and consultants. Participants were assigned to sections according to their interests, although several had to be reassigned in order to balance the number in the groups. Each of the participants was requested by letter to present in writing prior to the workshop a statement concerning his most serious problems or questions. This allowed the workshop chairman to establish his sections and place the section chairmen, recorders, consultants, and members accordingly.

Two problems only were considered by the workshop:

1. How relevant are our vocational training courses to employment demands in our respective areas; how can we better measure their relevance and look ahead to long-range employment situations?
2. How can we better integrate vocational training studies into high school and college programs in order to provide our trainees with sufficient academic skills should they wish to further their education?

Five sections were established, with three sections involved in the first problem and two sections concerned with the second problem.

The chairman of the workshop used the opening session to get everyone acquainted. The directors of the seven state departments introduced the participants from their respective states. The chairman then introduced the problems to be considered and assigned the participants to their sections.

Each section was asked to submit both their preliminary and final reports in a manner in which they could be read by the assembly. A specific form for all sections was agreed upon.

As the sections met, the chairman visited each several times to check on their progress, but unless he was asked to assist he was present only as an observer.

Following the preliminary reports, which were made by the section chairman or a delegated member, buzz sessions were used to consider the reports. The spokesmen for the buzz groups made suggestions while the recorder for the section kept notes of the suggestions offered by the assembly in order to incorporate the comments in the section's final report.

It is important that the schedule for the workshop remain flexible enough to allow for the difference in time necessary for the sections to complete their reports. The reports can be presented to the assembly in the order they are finished.

The final reports were considerd by the group as a whole, then further analyzed by the buzz groups before being adopted by the assembly.

The evaluation session at the end of the workshop was used to develop recommendations for the implementation of the workshop report, to discuss future workshop sessions, and to make plans for publishing the report.

Let us take a closer look at some of the factors which contributed to making this workshop a success.

Successful workshops

1. The workshop was planned cooperatively by persons who had a common problem and welcomed the holding of the workshop as a means of reaching a solution.

2. All persons in attendance participated in the planning of the workshop and played active roles while it was in session.

3. The workshop considered only two related problems.

4. There were no speakers and those with special knowledge were used as consultants while participating as members of the group.

5. The group processes utilized included sections assigned to various facets of the problems; the sections operated with leadership teams; section reports were presented verbally and in writing; general sessions were used for discussion; buzz sessions were used to analyze reports; observers checked on the progress of the sections; the chairman made himself available but did not intrude; an evaluation was made at the close of the workshop.

6. Time was provided for relaxation, for getting together with friends, or going out on the town.

7. The workshop chairman led the general sessions as a discussion leader. He involved the participants in all decisions and the group decided how, when, and in what fashion the reports were to be made.

8. The pace of the meeting continued until the end. Final reports were not allowed to drag along and the pace was enhanced by the use of the buzz groups. The final note was the evaluation session during which decisions were reached, recommendations for implementation made, and plans set for future workshops.

14 / Business staff meetings

One of the most difficult meetings to conduct is the business staff meeting. As the leader, you will be required to muster all your skills used in other types of meetings and be prepared to cope with situations peculiar to this type of group.

With the members of your staff you are the chief, the leader, the boss, and they are under your supervision. In a very real sense you are set apart from them regardless of how democratic you endeavor to be.

The members of your staff are geared differently than you for they have not had the responsibility for the section, division, department, or the firm. While they may accept responsibility for their own tasks, they, nevertheless, assume that the major problems are yours. Therefore, they are not used to thinking in terms of overall policy.

You may have discovered that your staff is more competitive than cooperative. They may be accustomed to struggling for position, for promotion, working to move ahead of the other staff members. As a result of this, there are bound to be suspicions, jealousies, conflicts which deter teamwork. There are likely to be feelings of insecurity on the part of some staff members, as well as repression of feelings.

You may find that your staff members are suspicious of your efforts to bring them into the planning stages, thinking, perhaps, that you are trying to pick their brains and taking the credit for it, or get them to do your work. Such attitudes may not exist or, if so, to only a slight degree and only occasionally, but it is well, nevertheless, to be alert and prepared to cope with these situations when they do occur.

As you think about your staff and your relationships with them, it would be well first to direct your attention to yourself. Ask yourself how effectual you are. How do you express your leadership? Would you be able to work efficiently under a leader such as yourself?

There are three types of leaders, frequently found in professional and business organizations, who have a difficult time working with others.

One of these types is the dictator, an able, efficient man who is dedicated to his responsibility but who finds it necessary to operate as a one-man show. Oftentimes these individuals are persons who started the business or built the department. They started alone and since have found it difficult to surrender any authority or delegate responsibility to others. They have to approve everything; nothing is done unless they give the green light. They never ask; they tell. What usually happens is they build corps of "yes men" around them for those are the only types of people who can work for them.

To learn to function in a democratic fashion would represent a big change for such men. Most of them do not see the advantage in changing and are not likely to be reading this or any other book on leadership. They believe they know it all.

The benevolent dictator makes an effort to be liked by his staff but he alone makes the decisions. Seeing himself somewhat in a fatherly role, he makes others dependent on him. His staff likes him and seeks his approval. Usually he is quick to praise but he views a failure as a personal affront. He talks about the team and the doing things together. Any discussions about the work, however, are solo.

Democratic leadership for this person is also a long shot for he believes that what he does is in the interest of everyone.

An exact opposite to the above types is the leader who forever avoids responsibility whenever possible. Obviously, he lacks confidence in himself and his ability to make decisions. His staff more or less do as they please while he appears to remain busy tampering with details. If he is the owner of the business, and it survives, it does so in spite of him and probably because someone else is the real leader and he is only the front man. Actually, this is the poorest leader of all, for lead is what he does not do. In all probability, his problems are greater than either the dictator or benevolent dictator and it will require a complete reconstruction of his personality in order for him to take hold as a real leader.

In contrast to these, the really effective leader is the democratic one, the leader who knows how and when to share responsibilities with his staff. He encourages leadership in others and he trains his staff to accept and handle responsibility.

English anthropologist Dr. Kilton Stewart, at the turn of the century, did a study on the Senois, a tribal people living in the heart of British Malaya. From the standpoint of leadership, he discovered that during the course of everyday living the tribesmen did pretty much as they pleased. Although they had no police force, they also had no crime and, yet, in view of this, they seemed to have no leadership. But Dr. Stewart noticed that when an emergency arose—the need for food, threats from a neighboring tribe—suddenly the elders of the community took over and the entire tribe formed ranks behind these leaders.

The ways in which a group functions determines the methods of leadership. As the leader, your awareness of this fact, along with suitable adjustments in the approach, can help you through problems which might otherwise result in failure.

The changes in the conditions and situations in which you operate may be frequent. Under most working conditions, at least, there are ups and downs, greater and lesser pressures. When we stop to think about it, it is really the element of change which requires leadership. So, in a very real way, your role is to serve as the catalyst whereby your staff can adapt to the changes and adjustments demanded of them.

Please note, however, that changes in the climate in which your staff must function don't necessarily call for a change in your leadership methods. A change is not necessary if your usual approach is suited to the demands called for by the change. This is particularly true if your leadership methods are flexible enough to provide sufficient leeway to meet most situations.

Major shifts in the conditions affecting your staff do require that you closely evaluate your methods. Let's take a look at some of the changes which might call for revisions.

Let's say, for example, that a fire breaks out in your industrial plant. Immediately you call for one employee to close the fire doors, another to distribute extinguishers, a third to reel out the fire hose, and so on. Such an emergency calls for rapid action and the autocratic approach is the natural one.

There are other moments less hectic than this caused, perhaps, by pressure on the staff by receiving an important rush order. There is a need for intensified effort and concentration of staff activity. It would appear that there is a direct connection between the amount of pressure and the need on the part of the staff for more guidance. In other words, in times of crisis people expect and seek stronger leadership. Effective leadership, then, usually coincides with what the staff feels is necessary.

There may be times when the nature of change faced by your staff is one where the usual course of business is replaced by conditions of uncertainty. This can occur when a company faces reorganization, a change of ownership, and so forth.

In this type of situation, personal relationships between yourself and your staff members require change. During the time that the fate or direction of the company hangs in the balance, you should make it your business to mingle with your staff as much as possible. Your personal contact with them can provide more reassurance than all the written or secondhand communiques can ever accomplish.

Remember, however, that a change in your approach requires an explanation or it will be upsetting. Otherwise your staff members may start saying to each other, "Things must be bad. The boss never acted this way before."

Changes can vary considerably in both degree and kind. The mechanisms or ways in which you adjust must depend on the nature of the change and the degree to which it affects your staff.

It has frequently been said that effective leadership resides in getting people to do what you want them to, when you want it done, and in the way you want it done, because they want to do it and because they have shared in deciding what, when, and how it is to be done.

If you accept this philosophy, then you will want to train yourself in the techniques of leading group discussion, as described earlier, in addition to paying close attention to the following:

Useful pointers

1. If you have decided to hold staff meetings, then plan to do it on a regular basis. Work with the staff on the scheduling, location, and length of the meetings, and hold them as planned. Calling meetings only when you feel like it will make your staff uneasy and suspicious of your motives.

2. Allow the staff to work with you in planning the agenda. While you will have some problems you feel are necessary to discuss, so will they. It works rather well to send a memo around listing some of the problems you wish to talk about and ask them to add their suggestions. You can then prepare the agenda from the returned memo.

3. When it comes time for your staff meeting, don't make the mistake of selecting the problems which you wish to discuss first and then following up with theirs if you have time. It would be wiser to share with the staff decisions as to the order of business. You can say, "All right, here is the agenda. What items would you like to consider first?" They may bring up matters which you consider to be of secondary importance, but the point is that you have taken a big step in making the staff feel that it is their meeting.

4. If you are going to ask the staff to share the responsibility and intend to follow through on decisions reached during staff meetings, then it is your job to see to it that the policies are enforced. Failure to follow through will indicate to staff members that the meetings are empty gestures. Such a result would be demoralizing to them, will affect your relationship with them, and subsequently will be reflected in the work record. Better not have staff meetings than to have this happen.

5. Keep your focus on ways in which you can make the best use of your staff members' talents. You will get to know your staff better than ever before and you will be able to recognize their abilities. You will discover the expeditors, the analyzers, evaluators, and, of course, the blockers and monopolizers. Members will emerge as leaders and you should give them the opportunity to lead, to take the chair, to lead discussions. As a member of the group, free of the responsibility of chairing the meeting, you will gain a new perspective of staff thinking. You needn't be concerned about losing status in surrendering the chair to others. Your position determines your status.

Show that you recognize the special knowledge of your staff members by asking them to serve as consultants when problems are being discussed in which they have particular expertise. Use your expeditors to take care of the physical arrangements. Rather than assign such tasks to the lowest person in the staff hierarchy, give the job to those who are good at it. Call attention to these talents. They will appreciate it and experience a greater security.

6. Committees can be used effectively if your staff is large enough to warrant them. Some work can be handled by committees rather than taking the time of the entire group. Appoint those who are interested in the committee's work and give them time to fulfill their assignments.

7. Don't allow the staff meetings to degenerate into gripe sessions. While it will be necessary to handle legitimate complaints, keep the focus and emphasis on improvements which can be made in the department, section, firm, or organization. Problems listed on

the agenda should be phrased in a manner that will direct the staff to think constructively rather than destructively.

8. The staff meeting can be an excellent means to sell your ideas to the staff. Sharing responsibility doesn't for a moment imply relinquishing leadership. As their leader, your staff members will expect you to have ideas and plans and they will appreciate the use of the staff meeting as the medium for this sharing. Following are some thoughts on ways to put your ideas across:

(a) Get the facts and present them when discussing your ideas.

(b) Have as your objective one on which they will agree and show that your plan will accomplish this objective.

(c) Reveal both the good and the bad, the strength and the weaknesses in your proposals. Present the holes before others discover them. This will tell them that you have thought your ideas through; nor will you be caught off guard on a weakness for which you have no answer.

(d) By presenting the arguments against your proposal first and finishing with the arguments in favor of it, they will be clearer on the positive side of the ledger and vaguer on the negative side.

9. Establish the habit in the staff meetings of clear, straight thinking on your part and that of others. One way to do this is to insist on the following considerations:

(a) Can the plan be carried out? Is it compatible with company policy and within the realm of possibility?

(b) Will the proposal accomplish what we want? Will it bring about improvements? Is it worth the efforts entailed?

(c) Do the facts justify what we propose to do?

If the decisions made by your staff will pass these tests, you will know they are on the right track.

By way of summarizing, then, successful staff meetings are the product of the following:

1. Your will and effort to give democratic leadership a chance to prove itself.

2. Your ability to handle the necessary techniques of effective group meetings.

3. Your effective use of the methods which specifically apply to business staff meetings.

15 / The successful leader

Do we cherish democracy because we believe in human beings as individuals; that people should participate in making decisions which will affect them individually and collectively; that individuals should have an opportunity to express their creative abilities; that people working together on common problems will come out with a better solution than any one of them could obtain alone?

Unless we, as interested and active citizens, learn to use the techniques of working together more effectively, many of the values which we hold dear in the democratic way of life will not be realized.

We must define and evaluate our beliefs about democracy. We must identify the behaviors which are essential for effective individual and group participation, and we must plan programs that will develop these behaviors as important outcomes for ourselves and others.

Some of the obstacles which have prevented the group process from operating effectively are: the tendency to accept policy from others without question; the attitude that group planning is too much trouble and too time consuming; delegating the power to another and letting him work it out; unfamiliarity of leaders with the group process.

Working effectively with others calls for a special kind of leader —one who helps the group to achieve its purposes and goals and the members to grow as a result of these experiences.

As a democratic leader, you are concerned with helping the members to work together, to make decisions, and to share responsibility. There will be times when you will give counsel and guidance to individuals and to the group. You may be a stimulating force, bringing about change in attitudes and interests, and you may be a teacher showing people how to do things and providing information in a creative way.

Techniques

As a successful leader, you will have a definite planned approach. The things that you will do are deliberate conscious efforts to influence the interaction so that goals can be realized. These efforts are generally referred to as techniques. They are something you say or do, such as a nod of your head, a gesture with your hand. If these things are done for the effect on an individual or a group, they are techniques. But a technique can also be something you refrain from doing. There will be times when you will not be sure of the reaction of the group and you may have to experiment with different techniques in order to gain the response you are seeking.

While applying these techniques, however, you must be sure that you are not trying to manipulate others. Techniques should be used only to initiate, or not initiate, chain reactions which will create a climate in which the work of the group can take place.

A friend of mine developed a rather interesting technique with his Boy Scout troop. He felt it contributed to their group experience and growth if he allowed sufficient time during each meeting for them to chat informally. When this was going on, he would sit with them and occasionally enter into the conversations. When he felt it was necessary to take control of the meeting and gain the attention of the group, he would stand in front of them. It worked very well for him and he seldom experienced any problems with discipline.

There are several principles which I consider to be necessary for effective leadership of most groups. Some of these principles are more relevant with some groups than others, but regardless of size, age, purpose, structure, or design, these principles will generally apply when working with people.

Principles

1. The leader should consider each member as an individual with needs, motives, abilities, and reasons for being a member of the group. As a leader, your success depends somewhat on learning about each person and making him feel important to the group.

2. Your group, organization, committee, commission, or whatever should be viewed by you as being unique, that its reason for being and its goals are important to the members, to the group as a whole, to the neighborhood, community, state, and even the nation. Just as each individual has needs, problems and motives, so does an organization. The health and ambition of the group is part of your responsibility.

3. There is a need for a continuous effort to achieve the integration of the members and the kind of unity that allows the knowledge, experience, and talent of the members to complement one another. If you, as the leader, can keep the focus of attention on the common denominators and the goals which can be realized only from working together, then petty disputes, jealousies, and small power struggles will be minimized. While a group of people working together can be compared to an orchestra, with each person playing his essential part, it must be remembered, however, that a group is not static. The roles played change, relationships change, people shift positions, with some growing and contributing more than others.

4. You should never delude yourself into believing that your ends—regardless of how noble or generous—can justify the means. As Mahatma Gandhi often pointed out to his followers, the ends cannot justify the means for the means are an end in themselves. How frequently and how sadly we have seen athletic coaches forget the importance of sportsmanship in order to gain the pride of coaching a winning team. How pathetic it is to see parents involved in a

children's theatre group lose sight of what their offspring could gain because of petty jealousies. How defeating it is to see the president of a service club use the organization to improve his own status in the community. Even the best intentions can go astray when things get out of focus.

A young man of my acquaintance was so interested in seeing the attendance grow at his church's youth fellowship meetings that he started offering games and refreshments as an incentive for attendance. New members came for the fun but matters quickly got out of hand as fun became the primary target. The steady, more serious members, who wanted to gain more than pleasure from the meetings, started attending the fellowship at another church.

Several years ago I was asked by the governor of Kansas to serve on a council to study the problems of delinquency and crime in Kansas. I was named to a committee on children's institutions. The chairman of this committee had an axe to grind: his only interest was using the committee to gain legislation for the construction of a minimum-security institution for youthful offenders. This was a worthy enough goal in itself but the point is that this man was so concerned with his target that he was determined to use the committee to gain it rather than allowing the group to come up with its own recommendations. Discovering that we could not function freely as a committee, we requested that the committee be dismissed and another committee formed.

5. You will want to remember that while the needs of the organization are your primary concern, you cannot overlook the needs of the individual members. It is fair to assume that the members have joined the organization to take part in the fulfillment of goals which they view as worthwhile. Nevertheless, the successful leader cannot ignore the fact that people also join groups for reasons of personal fulfillment. And it has been established time and again that those individuals who contribute the most are actually realizing fulfillment of their own personal needs. Divorce group goals from individual ones and you will be in serious trouble.

6. Your success as a leader depends in part upon how well you foster self-direction within the group. While certain obligations and

responsibilities are yours by virtue of your leadership, nevertheless, how well you have done your job is evidenced by how capably the group performs in your absence. The good leader is not one who promotes dependency on himself but rather one who so unifies the group and draws out individual talent that his absence does not undermine the effectiveness of the group.

In a democracy, decisions must be made by the people, not for them. This requires that people not only learn to govern their own lives, but must learn to function in group life and be able to reach decisions as a group. The democratic process is not an automatic one. People must learn to share responsibility through opportunities to experience it.

Teaching others to accept responsibility is not an easy task and sometimes it is so much easier just to do the job yourself. Particularly if you are working with children this is true, but you will not be fulfilling your role as a leader if you take this easier path. Obviously, your role is largely defined by the maturity and experience of those you are endeavoring to lead. If you are the chairman of a commission consisting of persons with knowledge and experiences similar to your own, your job may be somewhat as a moderator or catalyst. On the other hand, if you are working with a group of nine-year-olds, you cannot turn them loose to plan their own programs and activities. It will take work on your part to teach them responsibility and to involve them in the decision-making process.

7. You should make every effort to gain the participation and involvement of every member in the activities and program of the organization. As mentioned above, people join groups not only to fulfill the goals of the group but also to realize personal needs. If a member is not involved, he soon loses interest in the work of the organization which, in turn, suffers the loss of his support.

All of us have known individuals who revealed lukewarm attitudes toward the activities of groups and do a sudden reversal, displaying great enthusiasm, when invited to participate in activities meaningful to them. Everyone needs to feel wanted and appreciated. To be supportive of an organization, a member must believe he has a contribution which he can make toward its goals. It is a strange quirk of human nature to be critical of those activities from which he feels separated.

As a creative leader, you will not take for granted the roles which the group has assigned to its members. You should not assume that the present leaders—officers, committee chairmen—are the only members who have leadership abilities. It well may be that these quite unassuming persons simply have not had the opportunities to demonstrate their abilities. One of the biggest mistakes made by new leaders of old organizations with members of long tenure is to keep the same old group in director or leader roles. While the knowledge of these long-standing members should never be lost to the organization, keeping the same people in office year after year results in a kind of in-breeding which saps the strength of any organization.

8. It is well to remember that while the structure of an organization is the vital framework in which activities are carried out and goals are met, this structure is only the means whereby a group can achieve its objectives. The structure is the servant of the organization, not the master.

Of course, the structure, by-laws, purposes and goals of many organizations, clubs, associations are established at a national, district, or state level and a local chapter or branch has little to say in these matters. Nevertheless, within every group there are changes or innovations which can be made that will improve the climate, morale, or way of doing business.

It sometimes happens that when an organization is founded, its constitution and by-laws are quite adequate. Years later, however, the by-laws no longer meet the needs of the organization, yet they remain in effect, hampering the progress of the group. When this occurs, it is the responsibility of the leaders to change the by-laws in order to make them more relevant.

By-laws usually can be changed by a vote of the membership. If the by-laws of your organization can be changed only at the national or state level, and you are the leader of a local chapter, your first task is to determine whether the changes are desired by your members. If such be the case, your next step is to determine what procedures are necessary to introduce this matter before the national or state group. If you have followed the correct procedures and made your appeal in a diplomatic fashion and the parent group fails to present the matter to their directors or members, as they are obligated to do, then you are within your rights to appeal to other local groups for their support in gaining a national or state audience.

However, once your appeal for change is considered by the parent group and the appeal meets defeat, it is your obligation to live by this decision. There are no rules, of course, against your making additional appeals, collecting additional evidence, and strengthening your case. You can only justify such efforts, however, if you have the solid support of your own group.

In my experience, these principles can be useful to you in your functions as a leader. They are not so much rules as guidelines to help you find your direction. Quite obviously, their application and relevancy depends on the qualities of the leader, who must act out of his own experiences and judgment, and the type of organization being led, of which there are many varieties. Of great importance is the willingness to continue to learn from experience, take frequent inventory, and listen to others while doing your evaluations.

In fulfilling your various responsibilities, you can, for the most part, stay on the democratic bent. Now and then, however, you will discover the need to steer toward autocratic or laissez-faire extremes as the occasions demand. When the welfare or safety of the members is in danger, you may have to act in an autocratic manner, taking complete charge. At other times, you may be able to sit back as an observer and watch, allowing the group to make its own decisions.

Caution needs to be exercised in seeing that you are not too eager to take control under the guise that the members are not being responsible. On the other hand, you can be so anxious that the members shoulder responsibility that you are withdrawn when you should be more active.

While you may not always be conscious of this fact, as a leader you exercise a certain amount of power and regardless of how good your intentions are, there is always the possibility of its misuse.

Some leaders deliberately abuse their power. They strive to

exercise control over other people in order to solve their own problems. There are those who believe that most people are sheep, that they have to be told what to do. Dictatorial leaders believe this and it is a rationalization of their need to boss people in order to feel important themselves. Some leaders have excellent, unselfish goals for the group but they become so anxious to achieve their ends they lose sight of what is happening to the members along the way.

You should bear in mind that people do not always see things the way you do, so don't lose sight of the members' rights to differ with each other and with you. That is what democracy is all about. Conformity does not always mean balance and good adjustment. The majority can often be wrong.

Before concluding this chapter and the book, there are two other matters which I wish to mention to you. One has to do with the ability to reach decisions and the other matter has to do with the importance of personal influence. Both issues bear some importance to the tasks of leadership.

Reaching decisions

It is said that a donkey once starved between two haystacks because he could not choose between them. While the story implies that a donkey should be able to exercise choice, we most certainly know this is also true in the experiences of men.

People who are guilty of vacillation fail to put enough power behind their decisions and the smallest pressure brought to bear meets with little resistance. No "yes man" or "yes woman" long remains a leader. He or she is used by other people throughout their lives because both are easily manipulated. If placed in leadership roles, they are really only puppets whose strings are pulled by others.

Because many decisions are made emotionally or on impulse, careful consideration of all the factors involved has not been made. When the hasty choice has been made, other considerations immediately intrude; our decisions waver and soon are lost. There are times when one must choose between contradictory desires and the only question at such a time can be, "Which choice contributes the most to my overall goals?'' We can better meet temptation when we have firmly established guiding rules and principles to help us maintain control. Knowing what is right is not so hard to come by, but one has to work hard to develop the kind of self-discipline that will see us through the tough decisions. And discipline is probably the most important tool in the leader's box.

Choice can be simplified if viewed objectively and impersonally. Advise yourself as you would another person. Ask yourself if such-and-such a course will advance your goal in life? Will the benefits outweigh the disadvantages? Is it worth the sacrifice involved? Will my choice hinder or help others?

Choices are much easier to make and maintain if they grow out of a determined philosophy. If we have no philosophy, we have little foundation to guide us and if we do not know where we stand, how can others possibly follow our leadership?

To make a choice requires turning away from at least one other alternative. The story is told of how General Robert E. Lee chose integrity over both money and glamour. Following the Civil War, Lee was offered the presidency of a life insurance company at a salary of $25,000 a year. He told the directors of the company that he knew nothing about life insurance and wouldn't be worth a fraction of that amount. They replied that they didn't care whether he knew anything about insurance but what they were interested in was using his name. Whereupon Lee told them, "Well, gentlemen, if my name is so valuable, don't you think I should be very careful how it is used?'' Lee then accepted the presidency of a small college at an annual salary of $1,500.

Many famous leaders have been noted for their quick decisions, but these were more than likely much less impulsive than it would seem. First of all, their decisions were the result of predetermined policies and philosophies. Secondly, the decisions were probably the outcome of long preparation and careful consideration of facts. Only the delivery of the decision was sudden.

Where shortcuts in decision-making actually occur, they are the results of planning to anticipate crises or problems. The decision-maker pretty well knows in advance what action he will take when a certain situation arises. Some people, of course, never get out of the think tank. They are forever analyzing and in the meanwhile the time for action passes them by. In any case, they have not controlled the situation but have allowed things to happen to them. New information may change a decision, of course, but the additional data should be studied in reference to the original plan.

Oftentimes the greatest of wise decisions involves the discipline of patience. But waiting also must be active and not passive. To wait actively is to make selections, to exercise discrimination, to choose what you are waiting for,

It is not so difficult to choose between right and wrong, between good and evil. The tough decisions must be made between what appears to be two goods or the lesser of two evils. It is at such times that our predetermined policies and philosophies and our discipline come to our aid, for then we can say no, not only to those things which seem bad, but also to things which are pleasant, good, and profitable but which do not belong in our scheme of things at this time or under prevailing conditions.

Personal influence

Finally, let us consider this matter of the importance of personal influence on the lives of others.

The successful leader should realize that he probably will never know the full effect of his leadership on the members of his organization. Some of his success can be measured in the achievements of the group and the roles played by the members. Yet, it is the intangibles in your relationships with the members which will have the most influence upon their lives—what you are as a person, your understanding, your interest in them as individuals.

The name Curly Vaughn may not have been known outside the small town of Winfield, Kansas. He was not an ambitious man in the usual sense, so it made little difference to him. But to many of us who had the privilege of attending his classes and claiming him as a friend, he will always be one of the greatest men we have ever known.

Curly did not seek fame or recognition because he understood the simple yet profound secret of life that one's influence and most important contribution comes from bringing out the best in others. Whereas his own fame, had it been forthcoming, would have been short-lived, he was responsible for the success of many—a general, a well-known writer, a publisher of a national magazine, several college professors, clergymen, All-American athletes, physicians, and artists, to name a few.

He may not even have been considered the best of teachers by some since his lesson plans frequently fell behind schedule. Curly was not so much interested in science, his subject, as he was in the persons involved in the study. He demanded that the student understand himself and then relate this knowledge to the subject. If the student could not place himself within the experiment, Curly was not satisfied with the achievement.

On one occasion I overheard an argument between Curly and another teacher who was criticizing him for his delinquent schedule. "Hang it, man!" Curly retorted, "the lessons they'll forget, but if we teach them to think there isn't anything they can't learn!"

When talking about such matters as the color in a flower, he would point out that a tulip would reflect light waves, but that an observer was necessary for there to be color.

"*You* put the blue in the flower, you provide the color and the beauty," he would say.

Test tubes, slide rules, and graphs came alive under Curly's tutelage; they became part of our studies in English, part of our football game, part of our relationships with one another, part of our lives. And Curly was always there for those who needed him—before, between, and after classes, and at his home.

Perhaps the most valuable lesson we learned from Curly was never to underestimate the extent of our importance and our influence over others. "You are important because you are you, and there is no duplicate anywhere in the world. You have influence when you smile, influence when you cry, yawn, criticize, encourage."

Much of my work has been in the field of delinquency and crime, and I am sometimes tempted to seek shortcuts that do not exist for most social problems. Sometimes one wonders if anything will work.

Then, watching a psychiatrist quiet a disturbed child, a priest planting a seed of faith with the disheartened, a therapist helping a youngster to walk, a counselor restoring self-confidence in an alienated youth, a patrolman winning the respect of a once-tough gang, one remembers that social problems are solved only by persons working with persons, accepting the philosophy of being their brother's keeper, and having enough faith in their influence with others to dedicate their lives to the effort.

In my work I have frequent opportunities to talk with many church groups, service clubs, women's organizations, and youth groups. Quite frequently I am asked by these organizations what they can do to fight delinquency and crime or what useful youth project they can undertake.

This interest is indeed welcome, and one needs only to skim the record to discover that many worthwhile programs for children and youth are being accomplished by these institutions and organizations. Social and spiritual progress would certainly come to a standstill without the voluntary efforts of such dedicated groups.

While these institutions cannot function without their members, a person, however, cannot relieve himself of his individual responsibility to others only through his membership in groups. Individual responsibility is not so easily satisfied.

Curly would not allow us to excuse ourselves from our obligations so lightly. On one occasion he said to a popular student, "John, you participate in many school activities, and rightly so because you have intelligence and charm. These are fine gifts, and they bear great responsibilities, but they are in part wasted if you use them to gain only school honors and awards. There are many youngsters in this school who need your help, little things like paying attention to them, greeting them in the halls as an equal, encouraging them to do better, to stay in school, and to get involved in activities. They need someone like you to let them know they belong."

John went to work. Still in high school, he organized a youth group to keep students from dropping out of school. In college he established a student assistance committee for those threatened by failure. And today he is minister of a large church in Chicago where he carries on a personal evangelism with hard-to-reach youth.

Most of us have met a Curly Vaughn somewhere along the way as a teacher, neighbor, or friend of the family whose wisdom and understanding of human nature left an unforgettable image in the mind. And this is the point, for us to remember the persons who crossed our paths long after the particular surroundings or circumstances are long forgotten.

A young woman, who had been our neighbor, graduated from college last summer and took a job working in a slum section of New York. As she had grown up in a small Kansas town, I was curious as to how she would do in her first experience in the big city. This spring I had to go to New York on a business trip, so I decided to pay a visit to Carol. I found her in the playground surrounded by small youngsters, each trying to be the closest and gain the most attention. One small, dirty-faced little boy who was standing to one side of these activities turned to me and said, "Gosh, she's some pal!" It came from his heart and was the highest compliment he knew.

But later, talking to Carol about her work, I was surprised to learn that she was disappointed in her progress. When I asked why, she said, "They just yell and scream. I try but I can't keep them from doing it!"

Carol was discouraged because she could discover no immediate result in her influence. But how very great her influence was in the love and admiration these youngsters had for her. While Carol may never know, some of those little boys will be just a little bit kinder, speak a little bit softer, and seek just a little more from life because they knew Carol.

In the midst of great social upheavals, permanent goals seem elusive but one goal has remained unchanged, the recognition of the need for considerate and understanding persons. This is, above all else, the mark of a true leader.

Bibliography

Bales, R. F., and Borgatta, E. P. *Small Groups.* New York: Knopf, 1955.

Bandura, A., and Walters, R. H. *Social Learning and Personality Development.* New York: Holt, Rinehart & Winston, 1963.

Brown, A. C., and Geis, S. B. *Handbook For Group Leaders.* New York: Woman's Press, 1948.

Brown, J. F. *Psychology and the Social Order.* New York: McGraw-Hill, 1936.

Cartwright, D. C., and Zander, A. (Eds.). *Group Dynamics: Research and Theory.* New York: Harper & Row, 1968.

Cunningham, R., and Associates. *Understanding Group Behavior of Boys and Girls.* New York: Bureau of Publications, Teachers College, 1952.

Fiedler, F. E. *A Theory of Leadership Effectiveness.* New York: McGraw-Hill, 1967.

Freud, S. *Group Psychology and the Analysis of the Ego.* London & Vienna: International Psychoanalytic Press, 1922.

Gouldner, A. W. (Ed.). *Studies in Leadership.* New York: Harper, 1950.

Hastorf, A. H. *Research in Behavior Modification: New Developments and Implications.* New York: Holt, Rinehart & Winston, 1965.

Hemphill, J. K. *Leadership and Interpersonal Behavior.* New York: Holt, Rinehart & Winston, 1961.

Hollander, E. P. *Leaders, Groups and Influence.* New York: Oxford University Press, 1964.

Homans, G. C. *Social Behavior: Its Elementary Forms.* New York: Harcourt, Brace, & World, 1961.

Jennings, H. H. *Leadership and Isolation.* New York: Longmans, 1943.

Katz, D., and Kahn, R. *The Social Psychology of Organizations.* New York: Wiley, 1966.

McGrath, J. E., and Altman, I. *Small Group Research: A Critique and Synthesis of the Field.* New York: Holt, Rinehart & Winston, 1966.

McGregor, D. *The Human Side of Enterprise.* New York: McGraw-Hill, 1960.

McGregor, D. *Leadership and Motivation.* (Essays edited by W. G. Bennis and E. H. Schein). Cambridge, Massachusetts: M. I. T. Press, 1966.

Selznik, P. *Leadership in Administration.* Evanston: Row, Peterson, 1957.

Stogdill, R. M. *Individual Behavior and Group Achievement.* New York: Oxford University Press, 1959.

Weber, M. *The Theory of Social and Economic Organization.* (Trans. and ed. by T. Parsons and A. M. Henderson). New York: Oxford University Press, 1947.

Index

About the Author

Bill Schul is Kansas state director of the White House Conferences on Children and Youth.

He has served as a staff member in the Department of Preventative Psychiatry of the Menninger Foundation, as executive director of the Shawnee (Kansas) Community Mental Health Corporation, and as state director of the 7th Step Foundation.

He is founder of the Kansas Youth Council and past president of the Kansas City Council for Children and Youth.

"Accent on Youth," a column written by Mr. Schul, has appeared in 116 newspapers; he has also found time to write a biography, a book of poetry, and over one hundred articles for various magazines.

Mr. Schul earned a bachelor's degree in psychology from southwestern College, Winfield, Kansas, and a master's in English from the University of Denver.